The Cash Boy

The Cash Boy

By Horatio Alger Jr

DD BOOKS
Publishers for New Generations

The Cash Boy
by Horatio Alger Jr

Price: ₹ 250/-

ISBN: 9789359570501

DD Books
Delhi, India

www.ddbookshub.com
ddsalesglobal@gmail.com

Printed in the Republic of INDIA

Contents

Preface		7
Chapter–I.	Revelation	9
Chapter–II.	Mrs. Fowler's Story	14
Chapter–III.	Left Alone	19
Chapter–IV.	The Town Autocrat	22
Chapter–V.	A Little Misunderstanding	28
Chapter–VI.	Frank Gets a Place	31
Chapter–VII.	The Cash Boy has an Adventure	38
Chapter–VIII.	An Unexpected Engagement	44
Chapter–IX.	The Housekeeper's Nephew	48
Chapter–X.	The Housekeeper Scheming	53
Chapter–XI.	John Wade	60
Chapter–XII.	A False Friend	67
Chapter–XIII.	The Spider and the Fly	71
Chapter–XIV.	Springing the Trap	74
Chapter–XV.	From Bad to Worse	78

Chapter–XVI.	An Accomplice Found	85
Chapter–XVII.	Frank and his Jailer	90
Chapter–XVIII		93
Chapter–XIX.	What Frank Heard Through the Crevice	99
Chapter–XX.	The Escape	103
Chapter–XXI.	John Wade's Disappointment	109
Chapter–XXII.	Conclusion	114

Preface

"The Cash Boy," by Horatio Alger, Jr., as the name implies, is a story about a boy and for boys.

Through some conspiracy, the hero of the story when a baby, was taken from his relatives and given into the care of a kind woman.

Not knowing his name, she gave him her husband's name, Frank Fowler. She had one little daughter, Grace, and showing no partiality in the treatment of her children, Frank never suspected that she was not his sister. However, at the death of Mrs. Fowler, all this was related to Frank.

The children were left alone in the world. It seemed as though they would have to go to the poorhouse but Frank could not become reconciled to that.

A kind neighbor agreed to care for Grace, so Frank decided to start out in the world to make his way.

He had many disappointments and hardships, but through his kindness to an old man, his own relatives and right name were revealed to him.

Chapter-I
A Revelation

A group of boys was assembled in an open field to the west of the public schoolhouse in the town of Crawford. Most of them held hats in their hands, while two, stationed sixty feet distant from each other, were "having catch."

Tom Pinkerton, son of Deacon Pinkerton, had just returned from Brooklyn, and while there had witnessed a match game between two professional clubs. On his return he proposed that the boys of Crawford should establish a club, to be known as the Excelsior Club of Crawford, to play among themselves, and on suitable occasions to challenge clubs belonging to other villages. This proposal was received with instant approval.

"I move that Tom Pinkerton address the meeting," said one boy.

"Second the motion," said another.

As there was no chairman, James Briggs was appointed to that position, and put the motion, which was unanimously carried.

Tom Pinkerton, in his own estimation a personage of considerable importance, came forward in a consequential manner, and commenced as follows:

"Mr. Chairman and boys. You all know what has brought us together. We want to start a club for playing baseball, like the big clubs they have in Brooklyn and New York."

"How shall we do it?" asked Henry Scott.

"We must first appoint a captain of the club, who will have power to assign the members to their different positions. Of course you will want one that understands about these matters."

"He means himself," whispered Henry Scott, to his next neighbor; and here he was right.

"Is that all?" asked Sam Pomeroy.

"No; as there will be some expenses, there must be a treasurer to receive and take care of the funds, and we shall need a secretary to keep the records of the club, and write and answer challenges."

"Boys," said the chairman, "you have heard Tom Pinkerton's remarks. Those who are in favor of organizing a club on this plan will please signify it in the usual way."

All the boys raised their hands, and it was declared a vote.

"You will bring in your votes for captain," said the chairman.

Tom Pinkerton drew a little apart with a conscious look, as he supposed, of course, that no one but himself would be thought of as leader.

Slips of paper were passed around, and the boys began to prepare their ballots. They were brought to the chairman in a hat, and he forthwith took them out and began to count them.

"Boys," he announced, amid a universal stillness, "there is one vote for Sam Pomeroy, one for Eugene Morton, and the rest are for Frank Fowler, who is elected."

There was a clapping of hands, in which Tom Pinkerton did not join.

Frank Fowler, who is to be our hero, came forward a little, and spoke modestly as follows:

"Boys, I thank you for electing me captain of the club. I am afraid I am not very well qualified for the place, but I will do as well as I can."

The speaker was a boy of fourteen. He was of medium height for his age, strong and sturdy in build, and with a frank prepossessing countenance, and an open, cordial manner, which made him a general favorite. It was not, however, to his popularity that he owed his election, but to the fact that both at bat and in the field he excelled all the boys, and therefore was the best suited to take the lead.

The boys now proceeded to make choice of a treasurer and secretary. For the first position Tom Pinkerton received a majority of the votes. Though not popular, it was felt that some office was due him.

For secretary, Ike Stanton, who excelled in penmanship, was elected, and thus all the offices were filled.

The boys now crowded around Frank Fowler, with petitions for such places as they desired.

"I hope you will give me a little time before I decide about positions, boys," Frank said; "I want to consider a little."

"All right! Take till next week," said one and another, "and let us have a scrub game this afternoon."

The boys were in the middle of the sixth inning, when some one called out to Frank Fowler: "Frank, your sister is running across the field. I think she wants you."

Frank dropped his bat and hastened to meet his sister.

"What's the matter, Gracie?" he asked in alarm.

"Oh, Frank!" she exclaimed, bursting into tears. "Mother's been bleeding at the lungs, and she looks so white. I'm afraid she's very sick."

"Boys," said Frank, turning to his companions, "I must go home at once. You can get some one to take my place, my mother is very sick."

When Frank reached the little brown cottage which he called home, he found his mother in an exhausted state reclining on the bed.

"How do you feel, mother?" asked our hero, anxiously.

"Quite weak, Frank," she answered in a low voice. "I have had a severe attack."

"Let me go for the doctor, mother."

"I don't think it will be necessary, Frank. The attack is over, and I need no medicines, only time to bring back my strength."

But three days passed, and Mrs. Fowler's nervous prostration continued. She had attacks previously from which she rallied sooner, and her present weakness induced serious misgivings as to whether she would ever recover. Frank thought that her eyes followed him with more than ordinary anxiety, and after convincing himself that this was the case, he drew near his mother's bedside, and inquired:

"Mother, isn't there something you want me to do?"

"Nothing, I believe, Frank."

"I thought you looked at me as if you wanted to say something." "There is something I must say to you before I die."

"Before you die, mother!" echoed Frank, in a startled voice.

"Yes. Frank, I am beginning to think that this is my last sickness."

"But, mother, you have been so before, and got up again."

"There must always be a last time, Frank; and my strength is too far reduced to rally again, I fear."

"I can't bear the thought of losing you, mother," said Frank, deeply moved.

"You will miss me, then, Frank?" said Mrs. Fowler.

"Shall I not? Grace and I will be alone in the world."

"Alone in the world!" repeated the sick woman, sorrowfully, "with little help to hope for from man, for I shall leave you nothing. Poor children!"

"That isn't what I think of," said Frank, hastily.

"I can support myself."

"But Grace? She is a delicate girl," said the mother, anxiously. "She cannot make her way as you can."

"She won't need to," said Frank, promptly; "I shall take care of her."

"But you are very young even to support yourself. You are only fourteen."

"I know it, mother, but I am strong, and I am not afraid. There are a hundred ways of making a living."

"But do you realize that you will have to start with absolutely nothing? Deacon Pinkerton holds a mortgage on this house for all it will bring in the market, and I owe him arrears of interest besides."

"I didn't know that, mother, but it doesn't frighten me."

"And you will take care of Grace?"

"I promise it, mother."

"Suppose Grace were not your sister?" said the sick woman, anxiously scanning the face of the boy.

"What makes you suppose such a thing as that, mother? Of course she is my sister."

"But suppose she were not," persisted Mrs. Fowler, "you would not recall your promise?"

"No, surely not, for I love her. But why do you talk so, mother?" and a suspicion crossed Frank's mind that his mother's intellect might be wandering.

"It is time to tell you all, Frank. Sit down by the bedside, and I will gather my strength to tell you what must be told."

"Grace is not your sister, Frank!"

"Not my sister, mother?" he exclaimed. "You are not in earnest?"

"I am quite in earnest, Frank."

"Then whose child is she?"

"She is my child."

"Then she must be my sister—are you not my mother?"

"No, Frank, I am not your mother!"

Chapter-II
Mrs. Fowler's Story

Not my mother!" he exclaimed. "Who, then, is my mother?"

"I cannot tell you, Frank. I never knew. You will forgive me for concealing this from you for so long."

"No matter who was my real mother since I have you. You have been a mother to me, and I shall always think of you as such."

"You make me happy, Frank, when you say that. And you will look upon Grace as a sister also, will you not?"

"Always," said the boy, emphatically. "Mother, will you tell all you know about me? I don't know what to think; now that I am not your son I cannot rest till I learn who I am."

"I can understand your feelings, Frank, but I must defer the explanation till to-morrow. I have fatigued myself with talking, but to-morrow you shall know all that I can tell you."

"Forgive me for not thinking of your being tired, mother," and he bent over and pressed his lips upon the cheek of the sick woman. "But don't talk any more. Wait till to-morrow."

In the afternoon Frank had a call from Sam Pomeroy.

"The club is to play to-morrow afternoon against a picked nine, Frank," he said. "Will you be there?"

"I can't, Sam," he answered. "My mother is very sick, and it is my duty to stay at home with her."

"We shall miss you—that is, all of us but one. Tom Pinkerton said yesterday that you ought to resign, as you can't attend to your duties. He wouldn't object to filling your place, I fancy."

"He is welcome to the place as soon as the club feels like electing him," said Frank. "Tell the boys I am sorry I can't be on hand. They had better get you to fill my place."

"I'll mention it, but I don't think they'll see it in that light. They're all jealous of my superior playing," said Sam, humorously. "Well, good-bye, Frank. I hope your mother'll be better soon."

"Thank you, Sam," answered Frank, soberly. "I hope so, too, but she is very sick."

The next day Mrs. Fowler again called Frank to the bedside.

"Grace is gone out on an errand," she said, "and I can find no better time for telling you what I know about you and the circumstances which led to my assuming the charge of you."

"Are you strong enough, mother?"

"Yes, Frank. Thirteen years ago my husband and myself occupied a small tenement in that part of Brooklyn know as Gowanus, not far from Greenwood Cemetery. My husband was a carpenter, and though his wages were small he was generally employed. We had been married three years, but had no children of our own. Our expenses were small, and we got on comfortably, and should have continued to do so, but that Mr. Fowler met with an accident which partially disabled him. He fell from a high scaffold and broke his arm. This was set and he was soon able to work again, but he must also have met with some internal injury, for his full strength never returned. Half a day's work tired him more than a whole day's work formerly had done. Of course our income was very much diminished, and we were obliged to economize very closely. This preyed upon my husband's mind and seeing his anxiety, I set about considering how I could help him, and earn my share of the expenses.

"One day in looking over the advertising columns of a New York paper I saw the following advertisement:

"'For adoption—A healthy male infant. The parents are able to pay liberally for the child's maintenance, but circumstances compel them to delegate the care to another. Address for interview A. M.'

"I had no sooner read this advertisement than I felt that it was just what I wanted. A liberal compensation was promised, and under our present circumstances would be welcome, as it was urgently needed. I mentioned the matter to my husband, and he was finally induced to give his consent.

"Accordingly, I replied to the advertisement.

"Three days passed in which I heard nothing from it. But as we were sitting at the supper table at six o'clock one afternoon, there came a knock at our front door. I opened it, and saw before me a tall stranger, a man of about thirty-five, of dark complexion, and dark whiskers. He was well dressed, and evidently a gentleman in station.

"'Is this Mrs. Fowler?' he asked.

"'Yes, sir,' I answered, in some surprise

"'Then may I beg permission to enter your house for a few minutes? I have something to say to you.'

"Still wondering, I led the way into the sitting-room, where your father—where Mr. Fowler— —"

"Call him my father—I know no other," said Frank.

"Where your father was seated.

"'You have answered an advertisement,' said the stranger.

"'Yes, sir,' I replied.

"'I am A. M.,' was his next announcement. 'Of course I have received many letters, but on the whole I was led to consider yours most favorably. I have made inquiries about you in the neighborhood, and the answers have been satisfactory. You have no children of your own?'

"'No, sir.'

"'All the better. You would be able to give more attention to this child.'

"'Is it yours, sir?' I asked

"'Ye-es,' he answered, with hesitation. 'Circumstances,' he continued, 'circumstances which I need not state, compel me to separate from it. Five hundred dollars a year will be paid for its maintenance.'

"Five hundred dollars! I heard this with joy, for it was considerably more than my husband was able to earn since his accident. It would make us comfortable at once, and your father might work when he pleased, without feeling any anxiety about our coming to want.

"'Will that sum be satisfactory?' asked the stranger.

"'It is very liberal,' I answered.

"'I intended it to be so,' he said. 'Since there is no difficulty on this score, I am inclined to trust you with the care of the child. But I must make two conditions.'

"'What are they, sir?'

"'In the first place, you must not try to find out the friends of the child. They do not desire to be known. Another thing, you must move from Brooklyn.'

"'Move from Brooklyn?' I repeated.

"'Yes,' he answered, firmly. 'I do not think it necessary to give you a reason for this condition. Enough that it is imperative. If you decline, our negotiations are at an end.'

"I looked at my husband. He seemed as much surprised as I was.

"'Perhaps you will wish to consult together,' suggested our visitor. 'If so, I can give you twenty minutes. I will remain in this room while you go out and talk it over.'

"We acted on this hint, and went into the kitchen. We decided that though we should prefer to live in Brooklyn, it would be worth our while to make the sacrifice for the sake of the addition to our income. We came in at the end of ten minutes, and announced our decision. Our visitor seemed to be very much pleased.

"'Where would you wish us to move?' asked your father.

"'I do not care to designate any particular place. I should prefer some small country town, from fifty to a hundred miles distant. I suppose you will be able to move soon?'

"'Yes, sir; we will make it a point to do so. How soon will the child be placed in our hands? Shall we send for it?'

"'No, no,' he said, hastily. 'I cannot tell you exactly when, but it will be brought here probably in the course of a day or two. I myself shall bring it, and if at that time you wish to say anything additional you can do so.'

"He went away, leaving us surprised and somewhat excited at the change that was to take place in our lives. The next evening the sound of wheels was heard, and a hack stopped at our gate. The same gentleman descended hurriedly with a child in his arms—you were the child, Frank—and entered the house.

"'This is the child,' he said, placing it in my arms, 'and here is the first quarterly installment of your pay. Three months hence you will receive the same sum from my agent in New York. Here is his address,' and he placed a card in my hands. 'Have you anything to ask?'

"'Suppose I wish to communicate with you respecting the child? Suppose he is sick?'

"'Then write to A. M., care of Giles Warner, No. —— Nassau Street. By the way, it will be necessary for you to send him your postoffice address after your removal in order that he may send you your quarterly dues.'

"With this he left us, entered the hack, and drove off. I have never seen him since."

Chapter-III
Left Alone

Frank listened to this revelation with wonder. For the first time in his life he asked himself, "Who am I?"

"How came I by my name, mother?" he asked.

"I must tell you. After the sudden departure of the gentleman who brought you, we happened to think that we had not asked your name. We accordingly wrote to the address which had been given us, making the inquiry. In return we received a slip of paper containing these words: 'The name is immaterial; give him any name you please. A. M.'"

"You gave me the name of Frank."

"It was Mr. Fowler's name. We should have given it to you had you been our own boy; as the choice was left to us, we selected that."

"It suits me as well as any other. How soon did you leave Brooklyn, mother?"

"In a week we had made all arrangements, and removed to this place. It is a small place, but it furnished as much work as my husband felt able to do. With the help of the allowance for your support, we not only got on comfortably, but saved up a hundred and fifty dollars annually, which we deposited in a savings bank. But after five years the money stopped coming. It was the year 1857, the year of the great panic, and among others who failed was Giles Warner's agent, from whom we received our payments. Mr. Fowler went to New York to inquire about it, but only learned that Mr. Warner, weighed down by his troubles, had committed suicide, leaving no clew to the name of the man who left you with us."

"How long ago was that, mother?"

"Seven years ago nearly eight."

"And you continued to keep me, though the payments stopped."

"Certainly; you were as dear to us as our own child—for we now had a child of our own—Grace. We should as soon have thought of casting off her as you."

"But you must have been poor, mother."

"We were economical, and we got along till your father died three years ago. Since then it has been hard work."

"You have had a hard time, mother."

"No harder on your account. You have been a great comfort to me, Frank. I am only anxious for the future. I fear you and Grace will suffer after I am gone."

"Don't fear, mother, I am young and strong; I am not afraid to face the world with God's help."

"What are you thinking of, Frank?" asked Mrs. Fowler, noticing the boy's fixed look.

"Mother," he said, earnestly, "I mean to seek for that man you have told me of. I want to find out who I am. Do you think he was my father?"

"He said he was, but I do not believe it. He spoke with hesitation, and said this to deceive us, probably."

"I am glad you think so, I would not like to think him my father. From what you have told me of him I am sure I would not like him."

"He must be nearly fifty now—dark complexion, with dark hair and whiskers. I am afraid that description will not help you any. There are many men who look like that. I should know him by his expression, but I cannot describe that to you."

Here Mrs. Fowler was seized with a very severe fit of coughing, and Frank begged her to say no more.

Two days later, and Mrs. Fowler was no better. She was rapidly failing, and no hope was entertained that she would rally. She herself felt that death was near at hand and told Frank so, but he found it hard to believe.

On the second of the two days, as he was returning from the village store with an orange for his mother, he was overtaken by Sam Pomeroy.

"Is your mother very sick, Frank?" he asked.

"Yes, Sam, I'm afraid she won't live."

"Is it so bad as that? I do believe," he added, with a sudden change of tone, "Tom Pinkerton is the meanest boy I ever knew. He is trying to get your place as captain of the baseball club. He says that if your mother doesn't live, you will have to go to the poorhouse, for you won't have any money, and that it will be a disgrace for the club to have a captain from the poorhouse."

"Did he say that?" asked Frank, indignantly.

"Yes."

"When he tells you that, you may say that I shall never go to the poorhouse."

"He says his father is going to put you and your sister there."

"All the Deacon Pinkertons in the world can never make me go to the poorhouse!" said Frank, resolutely.

"Bully for you, Frank! I knew you had spunk."

Frank hurried home. As he entered the little house a neighbor's wife, who had been watching with his mother, came to meet him.

"Frank," she said, gravely, "you must prepare yourself for sad news. While you were out your mother had another hemorrhage, and—and—"

"Is she dead?" asked the boy, his face very pale.

"She is dead!"

Chapter-IV

The Town Autocrat

The Widder Fowler is dead," remarked Deacon Pinkerton, at the supper table. "She died this afternoon."

"I suppose she won't leave anything," said Mrs. Pinkerton.

"No. I hold a mortgage on her furniture, and that is all she has."

"What will become of the children?"

"As I observed, day before yesterday, they will be constrained to find a refuge in the poorhouse."

"What do you think Sam Pomeroy told me, father?"

"I am not able to conjecture what Samuel would be likely to observe, my son."

"He observed that Frank Fowler said he wouldn't go to the poorhouse."

"Ahem!" coughed the deacon. "The boy will not be consulted."

"That's what I say, father," said Tom, who desired to obtain his father's co-operation. "You'll make him go to the poorhouse, won't you?"

"I shall undoubtedly exercise my authority, if it should be necessary, my son."

"He told Sam Pomeroy that all the Deacon Pinkertons in the world couldn't make him go to the poorhouse."

"I will constrain him," said the deacon.

"I would if I were you, father," said Tom, elated at the effect of his words. "Just teach him a lesson."

"Really, deacon, you mustn't be too hard upon the poor boy," said his better-hearted wife. "He's got trouble enough on him."

"I will only constrain him for his good, Jane. In the poorhouse he will be well provided for."

Meanwhile another conversation respecting our hero and his fortunes was held at Sam Pomeroy's home. It was not as handsome as the deacon's, for Mr. Pomeroy was a poor man, but it was a happy one, nevertheless, and Mr. Pomeroy, limited as were his means, was far more liberal than the deacon.

"I pity Frank Fowler," said Sam, who was warm-hearted and sympathetic, and a strong friend of Frank. "I don't know what he will do."

"I suppose his mother left nothing."

"I understood," said Mr. Pomeroy, "that Deacon Pinkerton holds a mortgage on her furniture."

"The deacon wants to send Frank and his sister to the poorhouse."

"That would be a pity."

"I should think so; but Frank positively says he won't go."

"I am afraid there isn't anything else for him. To be sure, he may get a chance to work in a shop or on a farm, but Grace can't support herself."

"Father, I want to ask you a favor."

"What is it, Sam?"

"Won't you invite Frank and his sister to come and stay here a week?"

"Just as your mother says."

"I say yes. The poor children will be quite welcome. If we were rich enough they might stay with us all the time."

"When Frank comes here I will talk over his affairs with him," said Mr. Pomeroy. "Perhaps we can think of some plan for him."

"I wish you could, father."

"In the meantime, you can invite him and Grace to come and stay with us a week, or a fortnight. Shall we say a fortnight, wife?"

"With all my heart."

"All right, father. Thank you."

Sam delivered the invitation in a way that showed how strongly his own feelings were enlisted in favor of its acceptance. Frank grasped his hand.

"Thank you, Sam, you are a true friend," he said.

"I hadn't begun to think of what we were to do, Grace and I."

"You'll come, won't you?"

"You are sure that it won't trouble your mother, Sam?"

"She is anxious to have you come."

"Then I'll come. I haven't formed any plans yet, but I must as soon—as soon as mother is buried. I think I can earn my living somehow. One thing I am determined about—I won't go to the poorhouse."

The funeral was over. Frank and Grace walked back to the little house, now their home no longer. They were to pack up a little bundle of clothes and go over to Mr. Pomeroy's in time for supper.

When Frank had made up his bundle, urged by some impulse, he opened a drawer in his mother's bureau. His mind was full of the story she had told him, and he thought it just possible that he might find something to throw additional light upon his past history. While exploring the contents of the drawer he came to a letter directed to him in his mother's well-known handwriting. He opened it hastily, and with a feeling of solemnity, read as follows:

"My Dear Frank: In the lower drawer, wrapped in a piece of brown paper, you will find two gold eagles, worth twenty dollars. You will need them when I am gone. Use them for Grace and yourself. I saved these for my children. Take them, Frank, for I have nothing else to give you. The furniture will pay the debt I owe Deacon Pinkerton. There ought to be something over, but I think he will take all. I wish I had more to leave you, dear Frank, but the God of the Fatherless will watch over you—to Him I commit you and Grace.

"Your affectionate mother,

"RUTH FOWLER."

Frank, following the instructions of the letter, found the gold pieces and put them carefully into his pocketbook. He did not mention the letter to Grace at present, for he knew not but Deacon Pinkerton might lay claim to the money to satisfy his debt if he knew it.

"I am ready, Frank," said Grace, entering the room. "Shall we go?"

"Yes, Grace. There is no use in stopping here any longer."

As he spoke he heard the outer door open, and a minute later Deacon Pinkerton entered the room.

None of the deacon's pompousness was abated as he entered the house and the room.

"Will you take a seat?" said our hero, with the air of master of the house.

"I intended to," said the deacon, not acknowledging his claim. "So your poor mother is gone?"

"Yes, sir," said Frank, briefly.

"We must all die," said the deacon, feeling that it was incumbent on him to say something religious. "Ahem! your mother died poor? She left no property?"

"It was not her fault."

"Of course not. Did she mention that I had advanced her money on the furniture?"

"My mother told me all about it, sir."

"Ahem! You are in a sad condition. But you will be taken care of. You ought to be thankful that there is a home provided for those who have no means."

"What home do you refer to, Deacon Pinkerton?" asked Frank, looking steadily in the face of his visitor.

"I mean the poorhouse, which the town generously provides for those who cannot support themselves."

This was the first intimation Grace had received of the possibility that they would be sent to such a home, and it frightened her.

"Oh, Frank!" she exclaimed, "must we go to the poorhouse?"

"No, Grace; don't be frightened," said Frank, soothingly. "We will not go."

"Frank Fowler," said the deacon, sternly, "cease to mislead your sister."

"I am not misleading her, sir."

"Did you not tell her that she would not be obliged to go to the poorhouse?"

"Yes, sir."

"Then what do you mean by resisting my authority?"

"You have no authority over us. We are not paupers," and Frank lifted his head proudly, and looked steadily in the face of the deacon.

"You are paupers, whether you admit it or not."

"We are not," said the boy, indignantly.

"Where is your money? Where is your property?"

"Here, sir," said our hero, holding out his hands.

"I have two strong hands, and they will help me make a living for my sister and myself."

"May I ask whether you expect to live here and use my furniture?"

"I do not intend to, sir. I shall ask no favors of you, neither for Grace nor myself. I am going to leave the house. I only came back to get a few clothes. Mr. Pomeroy has invited Grace and me to stay at his house for a few days. I haven't decided what I shall do afterward."

"You will have to go to the poorhouse, then. I have no objection to your making this visit first. It will be a saving to the town."

"Then, sir, we will bid you good-day. Grace, let us go."

Chapter-V

A Little Misunderstanding

"Have you carried Frank Fowler to the poorhouse?" asked Tom Pinkerton, eagerly, on his father's return.

"No," said the deacon, "he is going to make a visit at Mr. Pomeroy's first."

"I shouldn't think you would have let him make a visit," said Tom, discontentedly. "I should think you would have taken him to the poorhouse right off."

"I feel it my duty to save the town unnecessary expense," said Deacon Pinkerton.

So Tom was compelled to rest satisfied with his father's assurance that the removal was only deferred.

Meanwhile Frank and Grace received a cordial welcome at the house of Mr. Pomeroy. Sam and Frank were intimate friends, and our hero had been in the habit of calling frequently, and it seemed homelike.

"I wish you could stay with us all the time, Frank—you and Grace," said Sam one evening.

"We should all like it," said Mr. Pomeroy, "but we cannot always have what we want. If I had it in my power to offer Frank any employment which it would be worth his while to follow, it might do. But he has got his way to make in the world. Have you formed any plans yet, Frank?"

"That is what I want to consult you about, Mr. Pomeroy."

"I will give you the best advice I can, Frank. I suppose you do not mean to stay in the village."

"No, sir. There is nothing for me to do here. I must go somewhere where I can make a living for Grace and myself."

"You've got a hard row to hoe, Frank," said Mr. Pomeroy, thoughtfully. "Have you decided where to go?"

"Yes, sir. I shall go to New York."

"What! To the city?"

"Yes, sir. I'll get something to do, no matter what it is."

"But how are you going to live in the meantime?"

"I've got a little money."

"That won't last long."

"I know it, but I shall soon get work, if it is only to black boots in the streets."

"With that spirit, Frank, you will stand a fair chance to succeed. What do you mean to do with Grace?"

"I will take her with me."

"I can think of a better plan. Leave her here till you have found something to do. Then send for her."

"But if I leave her here Deacon Pinkerton will want to put her in the poorhouse. I can't bear to have Grace go there."

"She need not. She can stay here with me for three months."

"Will you let me pay her board?"

"I can afford to give her board for three months."

"You are very kind, Mr. Pomeroy, but it wouldn't be right for me to accept your kindness. It is my duty to take care of Grace."

"I honor your independence, Frank. It shall be as you say. When you are able—mind, not till then—you may pay me at the rate of two dollars a week for Grace's board."

"Then," said Frank, "if you are willing to board Grace for a while, I think I had better go to the city at once."

"I will look over your clothes to-morrow, Frank," said Mrs. Pomeroy, "and see if they need mending."

"Then I will start Thursday morning—the day after."

About four o'clock the next afternoon he was walking up the main street, when just in front of Deacon Pinkerton's house he saw Tom leaning against a tree.

"How are you Tom?" he said, and was about to pass on.

"Where are you going?" Tom asked abruptly.

"To Mr. Pomeroy's."

"How soon are you going to the poorhouse to live?"

"Who told you I was going?"

"My father."

"Then your father's mistaken."

"Ain't you a pauper?" said Tom, insolently. "You haven't got any money."

"I have got hands to earn money, and I am going to try."

"Anyway, I advise you to resign as captain of the baseball club."

"Why?"

"Because if you don't you'll be kicked out. Do you think the fellows will be willing to have a pauper for their captain?"

"That's the second time you have called me a pauper. Don't call me so again."

"You are a pauper and you know it."

Frank was not a quarrelsome boy, but this repeated insult was too much for him. He seized Tom by the collar, and tripping him up left him on the ground howling with rage. As valor was not his strong point, he resolved to be revenged upon Frank vicariously. He was unable to report the case to his father till the next morning, as the deacon did not return from a neighboring village, whither he had gone on business, till late, but the result of his communication was a call at Mr. Pomeroy's from the deacon at nine o'clock the next morning. Had he found Frank, it was his intention, at Tom's request, to take him at once to the poorhouse. But he was too late. Our hero was already on his way to New York.

Chapter-VI

Frank Gets a Place

So this is New York," said Frank to himself, as he emerged from the railway station and looked about him with interest and curiosity.

"Black yer boots? Shine?" asked a bootblack, seeing our hero standing still.

Frank looked at his shoes. They were dirty, without doubt, but he would not have felt disposed to be so extravagant, considering his limited resources, had he not felt it necessary to obtain some information about the city.

"Yes," he said, "you may black them."

The boy was on his knees instantly and at work.

"How much do you make in a day?" asked Frank.

"When it's a good day I make a dollar."

"That's pretty good," said Frank.

"Can you show me the way to Broadway?"

"Go straight ahead."

Our hero paid for his shine and started in the direction indicated.

Frank's plans, so far as he had any, were to get into a store. He knew that Broadway was the principal business street in the city, and this was about all he did know about it.

He reached the great thoroughfare in a few minutes, and was fortunate enough to find on the window of the corner store the sign:

"A Boy Wanted."

He entered at once, and going up to the counter, addressed a young man, who was putting up goods.

"Do you want a boy?"

"I believe the boss wants one; I don't. Go out to that desk."

Frank found the desk, and propounded the same question to a sandy-whiskered man, who looked up from his writing.

"You're prompt," he said. "That notice was only put out two minutes ago."

"I only saw it one minute ago."

"So you want the place, do you?"

"I should like it."

"Do you know your way about the city?"

"No, sir, but I could soon find out."

"That won't do. I shall have plenty of applications from boys who live in the city and are familiar with the streets."

Frank left the store rather discomfited.

He soon came to another store where there was a similar notice of "A Boy Wanted." It was a dry goods store.

"Do you live with your parents?" was asked.

"My parents are dead," said Frank, sadly.

"Very sorry, but we can't take you."

"Why not, sir?"

"In case you took anything we should make your parents responsible."

"I shouldn't take anything," said Frank, indignantly.

"You might; I can't take you."

Our hero left this store a little disheartened by his second rebuff.

He made several more fruitless applications, but did not lose courage wholly. He was gaining an appetite, however. It is not surprising therefore, that his attention was drawn to the bills of a restaurant on the opposite side of the street. He crossed over, and standing outside, began to examine them to see what was the scale of prices. While in this position he was suddenly aroused by a slap on the back.

Turning he met the gaze of a young man of about thirty, who was smiling quite cordially.

"Why, Frank, my boy, how are you?" he said, offering his hand.

"Pretty well, thank you," said our hero bewildered, for he had no recollection of the man who had called him by name.

The other smiled a little more broadly, and thought:

"It was a lucky guess; his name is Frank."

"I am delighted to hear it," he continued. "When did you reach the city?"

"This morning," said the unsuspecting Frank.

"Well, it's queer I happened to meet you so soon, isn't it? Going to stay long?"

"I shall, if I can get a place."

"Perhaps I can help you."

"I suppose I ought to remember you," ventured our hero, "but I can't think of your name."

"Jasper Wheelock. You don't mean to say you don't remember me? Perhaps it isn't strange, as we only met once or twice in your country home. But that doesn't matter. I'm just as ready to help you. By the way, have you dined?"

"No."

"No more have I. Come in and dine with me."

"What'll you take?" asked Jasper Wheelock, passing the bill of fare to Frank.

"I think I should like to have some roast beef," said Frank.

"That will suit me. Here, waiter, two plates of roast beef, and two cups of coffee."

"How are they all at home?" asked Jasper.

"My mother has just died."

"You don't say so," said Jasper, sympathetically.

"My sister is well."

"I forgot your sister's name."

"Grace."

"Of course—Grace. I find it hard to remember names. The fact is, I have been trying to recall your last name, but it's gone from me."

"Fowler."

"To be sure Frank Fowler. How could I be so forgetful."

The conversation was interrupted by the arrival of the coffee and roast beet, which both he and his new friend attacked with vigor.

"What kind of pudding will you have?" asked the stranger.

"Apple dumpling," said Frank.

"That suits me. Apple dumpling for two."

In due time the apple dumpling was disposed of, and two checks were brought, amounting to seventy cents.

"I'll pay for both," said Jasper. "No thanks. We are old acquaintances, you know."

He put his hand into his pocket, and quickly withdrew it with an exclamation of surprise:

"Well, if that isn't a good joke," he said. "I've left my money at home. I remember now, I left it in the pocket of my other coat. I shall have to borrow the money of you. You may as well hand me a dollar!"

Frank was not disposed to be suspicious, but the request for money made him uneasy. Still there seemed no way of refusing, and he reluctantly drew out the money.

His companion settled the bill and then led the way into the street.

Jasper Wheelock was not very scrupulous; he was quite capable of borrowing money, without intending to return it; but he had his good side.

"Frank," said he, as they found themselves in the street, "you have done me a favor, and I am going to help you in return. Have you got very much money?"

"No. I had twenty dollars when I left home, but I had to pay my fare in the cars and the dinner, I have seventeen dollars and a half left."

"Then it is necessary for you to get a place as soon as possible."

"Yes; I have a sister to support; Grace, you know."

"No, I don't know. The fact is, Frank, I have been imposing upon you. I never saw you before in the whole course of my life."

"What made you say you knew me?"

"I wanted to get a dinner out of you. Don't be troubled, though; I'll pay back the money. I've been out of a place for three or four weeks, but I enter upon one the first of next week. For the rest of the week I've got nothing to do, and I will try to get you a place.

"The first thing is to get a room somewhere. I'll tell you what, you may have part of my room."

"Is it expensive?"

"No; I pay a dollar and a half a week. I think the old lady won't charge more than fifty cents extra for you."

"Then my share would be a dollar."

"You may pay only fifty cents. I'll keep on paying what I do now. My room is on Sixth Avenue." They had some distance to walk. Finally Jasper halted before a baker's shop.

"It's over this," he said.

He drew out a latch-key and entered.

"This is my den," he said. "It isn't large you can't get any better for the money."

"I shall have to be satisfied," said Frank. "I want to get along as cheap as I can."

"I've got to economize myself for a short time. After this week I shall earn fifteen dollars a week."

"What business are you in, Mr. Wheelock?"

"I am a journeyman printer. It is a very good business, and I generally have steady work. I expect to have after I get started again. Now, shall I give you some advice?"

"I wish you would."

"You don't know your way around New York. I believe I have a map somewhere. I'll just show you on it the position of the principal streets, and that will give you a clearer idea of where we go."

The map was found and Jasper explained to Frank the leading topographical features of the Island City.

One thing only was wanting now to make him contented, and this was employment. But it was too late to make any further inquiries.

"I've been thinking, Frank," said Jasper, the next morning, "that you might get the position as a cash-boy."

"What does a cash-boy do?"

"In large retail establishments every salesman keeps a book in which his sales are entered. He does not himself make change, for it would not do to have so many having access to the money-drawer. The money is carried to the cashier's desk by boys employed for the purpose, who return with the change."

"Do you think I can get a situation as cash-boy?"

"I will try at Gilbert & Mack's. I know one of the principal salesmen. If there is a vacancy he will get it for you to oblige me."

They entered a large retail store on Broadway. It was broad and spacious. Twenty salesmen stood behind the counter, and boys were running this way and that with small books in their hands.

"How are you, Duncan?" said Jasper.

The person addressed was about Jasper Wheelock's age. He had a keen, energetic look and manner, and would be readily singled out as one of the leading clerks.

"All right, Wheelock. How are you?" he responded. "Do you want anything in our line?"

"No goods; I want a place for this youngster. He's a friend of mine. I'll answer for his good character."

"That will be satisfactory. But what sort of a place does he want?"

"He is ready to begin as cash-boy."

"Then we can oblige you, as one of our boys has fallen sick, and we have not supplied his place. I'll speak to Mr. Gilbert."

He went up to Mr. Gilbert, a portly man in the back part of the store. Mr. Gilbert seemed to be asking two or three questions. Frank waited the result in suspense, dreading another disappointment, but this time he was fortunate.

"The boy can stay," reported Duncan. "His wages are three dollars a week."

It was not much, but Frank was well pleased to feel that at last he had a place in the city.

He wrote a letter to Grace in the evening, announcing his success, and expressing the hope that he would soon be able to send for her.

Chapter-VII

The Cash Boy has an Adventure

Four weeks passed. The duties of a cash-boy are simple enough, and Frank had no difficulty in discharging them satisfactorily. At first he found it tiresome, being on his feet all day, for the cash-boys were not allowed to sit down, but he got used to this, being young and strong.

All this was very satisfactory, but one thing gave Frank uneasiness. His income was very inadequate to his wants.

"What makes you so glum, Frank?" asked Jasper Wheelock one evening.

"Do I look glum?" said Frank. "I was only thinking how I could earn more money. You know how little I get. I can hardly take care of myself, much less take care of Grace."

"I can lend you some money, Frank. Thanks to your good advice, I have got some laid up."

"Thank you, Jasper, but that wouldn't help matters. I should owe you the money, and I don't know how I could pay you."

"About increasing your income, I really don't know," said Jasper. "I am afraid Gilbert & Mack wouldn't raise your wages."

"I don't expect it. All the rest of the cash-boys would ask the same thing."

"True; still I know they are very well pleased with you. Duncan told me you did more work than any of the rest of the boys."

"I try to do all I can."

"He said you would make a good salesman, he thought. Of course you are too young for that yet."

"I suppose I am."

"Frank, I am earning fifteen dollars a week, you know, and I can get along on ten, but of the five I save let me give you two. I shall never feel it, and by and by when you are promoted it won't be necessary."

"Jasper, you are a true friend," said Frank, warmly; "but it wouldn't be right for me to accept your kind offer, though I shan't forget it. You have been a good friend to me."

"And you to me, Frank. I'll look out for you. Perhaps I may hear of something for you."

Small as Frank's income was, he had managed to live within it. It will be remembered that he had paid but fifty cents a week for a room. By great economy he had made his meals cost but two dollars a week, so that out of his three dollars he saved fifty cents. But this saving would not be sufficient to pay for his clothes. However, he had had no occasion to buy any as yet, and his little fund altogether amounted to twenty dollars. Of this sum he inclosed {sic} eight dollars to Mr. Pomeroy to pay for four weeks' board for Grace.

"I hope I shall be able to keep it up," he said to himself, thoughtfully. "At any rate, I've got enough to pay for six weeks more. Before that time something may turn up."

Several days passed without showing Frank any way by which he could increase his income. Jasper again offered to give him two dollars a week out of his own wages, but this our hero steadily refused.

One Friday evening, just as the store was about to close, the head salesman called Frank to him.

"Where do you live?" he asked.

"In Sixth avenue, near Twenty-fifth street."

"There's a bundle to go to Forty-sixth street. I'll pay your fare upon the stage if you'll carry it. I promised to send it to-night, and I don't like to disappoint the lady."

"I can carry it just as well as not."

Frank took the bundle, and got on board a passing omnibus. There was just one seat vacant beside an old gentleman of seventy, who appeared to be quite feeble.

At Forty-fifth street he pulled the strap and prepared to descend, leaning heavily on his cane as he did so. By some mischance the horses started a little too soon and the old man, losing his footing, fell in the street. Frank observed the accident and sprang out instantly to his help.

"I hope you are not much hurt, sir?" he said, hastily.

"I have hurt my knee," said the old gentleman.

"Let me assist you, sir," said Frank, helping him up.

"Thank you, my boy. I live at number forty-five, close by. If you will lead me to the door and into the house I shall be much indebted to you."

"Certainly, sir. It is no trouble to me."

With slow step, supported by our hero, the old gentleman walked to his own door.

It was opened by a maid servant, who looked with some surprise at Frank.

"I fell, Mary," explained her master, "and this young gentleman has kindly helped me home."

"Did you hurt yourself much, sir?"

"Not seriously."

"Can I do anything more for you, sir?" asked Frank.

"Come in a moment."

Our hero followed his new acquaintance into a handsomely furnished parlor.

"Now, my young friend tell me if you have been taken out of your way by your attention to me?"

"Oh, no, sir; I intended to get out at the next street."

"My dinner is just ready. Won't you stop and dine with me?"

"Thank you, sir," he said, hesitatingly, "but I promised to carry this bundle. I believe it is wanted at once."

"So you shall. You say the house is in the next street. You can go and return in five minutes. You have done me a service, and I may have it in my power to do something for you in return."

"Perhaps," thought Frank, "he can help me to some employment for my evenings." Then, aloud:

"Thank you, sir; I will come."

Five minutes later Frank was ushered into a handsome dining-room. The dinner was already on the table, but chairs were only set for three. The one at the head of the table was of course occupied by the old gentleman, the one opposite by Mrs. Bradley, his housekeeper, and one at the side was placed for Frank.

"Mrs. Bradley," said the old gentleman, "this is a young gentleman who was kind enough to help me home after the accident of which I just spoke to you. I would mention his name, but I must leave that to him."

"Frank Fowler, sir."

"And my name is Wharton. Now that we are all introduced, we can talk more freely."

"Will you have some soup, Mr. Fowler?" asked the housekeeper.

She was a tall thin woman, with a reserved manner that was somewhat repellant. She had only nodded slightly at the introduction, fixing her eyes coldly and searchingly on the face of our hero. It was evident that whatever impression the service rendered might have made upon the mind of Mr. Wharton, it was not calculated to warm the housekeeper to cordiality.

"Thank you," he answered, but he could not help feeling at the same time that Mrs. Bradley was not a very agreeable woman.

"You ought to have a good appetite," said Mr. Wharton. "You have to work hard during the day. Our young friend is a cash-boy at Gilbert & Mack's, Mrs. Bradley.

"Oh, indeed!" said Mrs. Bradley, arching her brows as much as to say: "You have invited strange company to dinner."

"Do your parents live in the city, Frank—I believe your name is Frank?"

"No, sir; they are dead. My mother died only a few weeks since."

"And have you no brothers and sisters?"

"I have one sister—Grace."

"I suppose she is in the city here with you?"

"No, sir. I left her in the country. I am here alone."

"I will ask you more about yourself after dinner. If you have no engagement, I should like to have you stay with me a part of the evening."

"Thank you, sir."

Frank accepted the invitation, though he knew Jasper would wonder what had become of him. He saw that the old gentleman was kindly disposed toward him, and in his present circumstances he needed such a friend.

But in proportion as Mr. Wharton became more cordial, Mrs. Bradley became more frosty, until at last the old gentleman noticed her manner.

"Don't you feel well this evening, Mrs Bradley?" he asked.

"I have a little headache," said the housekeeper, coldly.

"You had better do something for it."

"It will pass away of itself, sir."

They arose from the dinner table, and Mr. Wharton, followed by Frank, ascended the staircase to the front room on the second floor, which was handsomely fitted up as a library.

"What makes him take such notice of a mere cash-boy?" said Mrs. Bradley to herself. "That boy reminds me of somebody. Who is it?"

Chapter-VIII
An Unexpected Engagement

"Take a seat, Frank," said Mr. Wharton, pointing to a luxurious armchair on one side of the cheerful grate fire; "I will take the other, and you shall tell me all about yourself."

"Thank you, sir," said our hero.

His confidence was won by Mr. Wharton's kind tone, and he briefly recounted his story.

At the conclusion, Mr. Wharton said:

"How old are you, Frank?"

"Fourteen, sir."

"You are a brave boy, and a good boy, and you deserve success."

"Thank you, sir."

"But I am bound to say that you have a hard task before you."

"I know it, sir."

"Why not let your sister go to the poorhouse for a few years, till you are older, and better able to provide for her?"

"I should be ashamed to do it, sir," he said. "I promised my mother to take care of Grace, and I will."

"How much do you earn as a cash-boy?"

"Three dollars a week."

"Only three dollars a week! Why, that won't pay your own expenses!" said the old gentleman in surprise.

"Yes, sir, it does. I pay fifty cents a week for my room, and my meals don't cost me much."

"But you will want clothes."

"I have enough for the present, and I am laying up fifty cents a week to buy more when I need them."

"You can't buy many for twenty-six dollars a year. But that doesn't allow anything for your sister's expenses."

"That is what puzzles me, sir," said Frank, fixing a troubled glance upon the fire. "I shall have to work in the evenings for Grace."

"What can you do?"

"I could copy, but I suppose there isn't much chance of getting copying to do."

"Then you have a good handwriting?"

"Pretty fair, sir."

"Let me see a specimen. There are pen and ink on the table, and here is a sheet of paper."

Frank seated himself at the table, and wrote his name on the paper.

"Very good," said his host, approvingly. "Your hand is good enough for a copyist, but you are correct in supposing that work of that kind is hard to get. Are you a good reader?"

"Do you mean in reading aloud, sir?"

"Yes."

"I will try, if you wish."

"Take a book from the table—any book—and let me hear you read."

Frank opened the first book that came to hand—one of Irving's and read in a clear, unembarrassed voice about half a page.

"Very good indeed!" said Mr. Wharton. "You have been well taught. Where did you attend school?"

"Only in the town school, sir."

"You have, at any rate, made good use of your advantages."

"But will it do me any good, sir?" asked Frank.

"People are not paid for reading, are they?"

"Not in general, but we will suppose the case of a person whose eyes are weak, and likely to be badly affected by evening use. Then suppose such a person could secure the services of a good, clear, distinct reader, don't you think he would be willing to pay something?"

"I suppose so. Do you know of any such person?" asked Frank.

"I am describing myself, Frank. A year since I strained my eyes very severely, and have never dared to use them much since by gaslight. Mrs. Bradley, my housekeeper, has read to me some, but she has other duties, and I don't think she enjoys it very much. Now, why shouldn't I get you to read to me in the evening when you are not otherwise employed?"

"I wish you would, Mr. Wharton," said Frank, eagerly. "I would do my best."

"I have no doubt of that, but there is another question—perhaps you might ask a higher salary than I could afford to pay."

"Would a dollar a week be too much?" asked Frank.

"I don't think I could complain of that," said Mr. Wharton, gravely. "Very well, I will engage you as my reader."

"Thank you, sir."

"But about the pay; I have made up my mind to pay you five dollars a week."

"Five dollars a week!" Frank repeated. "It is much more than my services will be worth sir."

"Let me judge of that, Frank."

"I don't know how to thank you, sir," said Frank, gratefully. "I never expected to be so rich. I shall have no trouble in paying for Grace's board and clothes now. When do you want me to begin reading to you?"

"You may as well begin to-night—that is, unless you have some other engagement."

"Oh, no, sir, I have nothing else to do."

"Take the Evening Post, then, and read me the leading editorial. Afterward, I will tell you what to read."

Frank had been reading about half an hour, when a knock was heard at the door.

"Come in," said Mr. Wharton.

Mrs. Bradley entered, with a soft, quiet step.

"I thought, sir," she began, "you might like me to read to you, as usual."

"Thank you, Mrs. Bradley, but I am going to relieve you of that portion of your labors. My young friend here is to come every evening and read to me."

"Indeed!" ejaculated the housekeeper in a tone of chilly displeasure, and a sharp glance at Frank, which indicated no great amount of cordiality. "Then, as I am intruding, I will take my leave."

There was something in her tone that made Frank feel uncomfortable.

Chapter-IX

The Housekeeper's Nephew

By no means," said Mr. Wharton, as the housekeeper was about to withdraw; "don't imagine you are intruding. Come in and sit down."

"Thank you, sir," said Mrs. Bradley, in a measured tone. "You are very considerate, I am sure, but if you'll excuse me, I won't come in this evening."

"Mrs. Bradley has been with me a good many years," explained Mr. Wharton, "and I dare say she feels a little disturbed at seeing another occupy her place, even in a duty like this."

"I am afraid she will be offended with me, sir," said Frank.

"Oh, no; I will explain matters to her. Go on with your reading, Frank."

At half-past nine, Mr. Wharton took out his watch.

"It is getting late," he said. "I have no doubt you are tired and need rest."

"I am not tired, sir."

"I believe in going to bed early. I shall seldom keep you later than this. Do you think you can find your way out?"

"Yes, sir. When shall I come to-morrow evening?"

"A little before eight."

"I will be punctual."

Jasper was waiting for him, not wholly without anxiety, for it was very unusual for Frank to be late.

"Well, Frank!" he exclaimed; "this is a pretty time for you to come home. I began to think you had got into trouble. I was just going around to the nearest station house in search of you."

"I was in quite a different place, Jasper."

Frank told his story, including an account of his engagement.

"So it seems I am to lose your company in the evening. I am sorry for that, but I am glad you are so lucky."

"It was better than I expected," said Frank, with satisfaction.

"What sort of a man is this Mr. Wharton?" said Jasper.

"He is very kind and generous. I am lucky to have so good a friend. There's only one thing that is likely to be disagreeable."

"What's that?"

"The housekeeper—her name is Mrs. Bradley—for some reason or other she doesn't want me there."

"What makes you think so?"

"Her manner, and the way she speaks. She came in to read to Mr. Wharton last evening, and didn't seem to like it because I had been taken in her place."

"She is evidently jealous. You must take care not to offend her. She might endeavor to have you dismissed."

"I shall always treat her politely, but I don't think I can ever like her."

Meanwhile, the housekeeper, on leaving the library, had gone to her own room in dudgeon.

"Mr. Wharton's a fool!" she muttered to herself.

"What possessed him to take this cash-boy from the streets, invite him to dinner, and treat him as an honored guest, and finally to engage him as a reader? I never heard of anything so ridiculous! Is this little vagabond to take my place in the old man's good graces? I've been slaving and slaving for twenty years, and what have I got by it? I've laid up two thousand dollars; and what is that to provide for my old age? If the old man would die, and remember me handsomely in his will, it would be worth while; but this new favorite may stand in my way. If he does I'll be revenged on him as sure as my name is Ulrica Bradley."

Here the area bell rang, and in a moment one of the housemaids entered Mrs. Bradley's room.

"There's your nephew outside, ma'am, and wanting to see you."

"Tell him to come in," and the housekeeper's cold face became softer and pleasanter in aspect as a young man of twenty entered and greeted her carelessly.

"How are you, aunt?"

"Pretty well, Thomas," she answered. "You haven't been here for some time."

"No. I've had a lot of work to do. Nothing but work, work, all the time," he grumbled. "I wish I was rich."

"You get through at six o'clock, don't you?"

"Yes."

"I hope you spend your evenings profitably, Thomas?"

"I ain't likely to go on any sprees, aunt, if that's what you mean. I only get twelve dollars a week."

"I should think you might live on it."

"Starve, you mean. What's twelve dollars to a young fellow like me when he's got his board to pay, and has to dress like a gentleman?"

"You are not in debt, I hope, Thomas?" said Mrs. Bradley, uneasily.

"I owe for the suit I have on, and I don't know where I'm going to get the money to pay for it."

He was dressed in a flashy style, not unlike what is popularly denominated a swell. His coarse features were disfigured with unhealthy blotches, and his outward appearance was hardly such as to recommend him. But to him alone the cold heart of the housekeeper was warm. He was her sister's son and her nearest relative. Her savings were destined for him, and in her attachment she was not conscious of his disagreeable characteristics. She had occasionally given him a five-dollar bill to eke out what he termed his miserable pay, and now whenever he called he didn't spare hints that he was out of pocket, and that a further gift would be acceptable. Indeed, the only tie that bound him to his aunt was a mercenary one.

But the housekeeper, sharp-sighted as she ordinarily was, did not detect the secret motive of such attention she received from her nephew. She flattered herself that he really loved her, not suspecting that he was too selfish to love anybody but himself.

"Thomas," she said, with a sudden thought, "I may be able to help you to an increase of your income. Mr. Wharton needs somebody to read to him evenings. On my recommendation he might take you."

"Thank you, aunt, but I don't see it. I don't want to be worked to death."

"But, think, Thomas," said his aunt, earnestly. "He is very rich. He might take a fancy to you and remember you in his will."

"I wish somebody would remember me in his will. Do you really think there's any chance of the old boy's doing something handsome for me?"

"That depends on yourself. You must try to please him."

"Well, I must do something. What'll he give?"

"I don't know yet. In fact, there's another reading to him just now."

"Then there's no chance for me."

"Listen to me. It's a boy he's picked up in the streets, quite unsuited for the place. He's a cash-boy at Gilbert & Mack's. Why, that's where you are," she added, with sudden recollection.

"A cash-boy from my own place? What's his name?"

"Fowler, I believe."

"I know him—he's lately come. How did he get in with the old man?"

"Mr. Wharton fell in the street, and he happened to be near, and helped him home."

"You'll have to manage it, aunt."

"I'll see what I can do to-morrow. He ought to prefer my nephew to a strange boy, seeing I have been twenty years in his service. I'll let you know as soon as I have accomplished anything."

"I don't half like the idea of giving up my evenings. I don't believe I can stand it."

"It is only for a little while, to get him interested in you."

"Maybe I might try it a week, and then tell him my health was failing, and get him to do something else for me."

"At any rate, the first thing must be to become acquainted."

Thomas now withdrew, for he did not enjoy spending an evening with his aunt, the richer by five dollars, half of which was spent before the evening closed at a neighboring billiard saloon.

Chapter-X

The Housekeeper Scheming

If Mrs. Bradley had been wiser, she would have felt less confident of her nephew's producing a favorable impression upon Mr. Wharton. She resolved to open the subject at the breakfast table.

"I didn't know, Mr. Wharton," she commenced, "that you intended to engage a reader."

"Nor did I propose to do so until last evening."

"I think—you'll excuse me for saying so—that you will find that boy too young to suit you."

"I don't think so. He reads very clearly and distinctly."

"If I had known you thought of engaging a reader, I would have asked you to engage my nephew."

"Indeed, I was not aware that you had a nephew in the city. Is he a boy?"

"No; he is a young man. He was twenty years old last June."

"Is he unfavorably situated?"

"He has a place as salesman."

"With what firm?"

"Gilbert & Mack."

"Why, that is the same firm that employs my young friend. It is a good firm."

"Perhaps it is, but my poor nephew receives a very small salary. He finds it very hard to get along."

"Your nephew is young. He will be promoted if he serves his employers well."

"Thomas would have been glad to read to you in the evening, sir," said Mrs. Bradley, commencing the attack.

"But for my present engagement, I might have taken him," said Mr. Wharton, politely.

"Have you engaged that boy for any length of time?"

"No; but it is understood that he will stay while I need him, and he continues to suit me. I have a favorable opinion of him. Besides, he needs the pay. He receives but three dollars a week as a cash-boy, and has a sister to support as well as himself."

"I am sorry," she said in an injured tone. "I hope you'll excuse my mentioning it, but I took the liberty, having been for twenty years in your employ."

"To be sure! You were quite right," said her employer, kindly. "Perhaps I may be able to do something for your nephew, though not that. Tell him to come and see me some time."

"Thank you, sir," said the housekeeper.

There was one question she wanted to determine, and that was the amount of compensation received by Frank. She did not like to inquire directly from Mr. Wharton, but resolved to gain the information from our hero. Some evenings later she had the opportunity. Mr. Wharton had an engagement, and asked her to tell Frank, when he arrived that he was released from duty. Instead of this she received him in the library herself.

"Probably Mr. Wharton will not be at home this evening," she said. "If he does not return in half an hour, you need not wait."

She took up her work, seated in Mr. Wharton's usual place, and Frank remained ready for duty.

"Mr. Wharton tells me you have a sister," she said.

"Yes, ma'am."

"You must find it hard work to provide for her as well as yourself."

"I do, or rather I did till I came here."

"How much does Mr. Wharton pay you?" she asked, in an indifferent tone.

"Five dollars a week," answered Frank.

"You are lucky that you have such a chance," she said.

"Yes, ma'am; it is more than I earn, I know, but it is a great help to me."

"And how much do you get as cash-boy?"

"Three dollars a week."

"So you actually receive nearly twice as much for a couple of hours in the evening as for the whole day."

"Yes, ma'am."

"What a pity Thomas can't have this chance," she thought.

When it was nine o'clock, she said:

"You need not wait any longer. Mr. Wharton will not be home in time to hear you read."

"Good-evening, Mrs. Bradley," said Frank.

"Good-evening!" she responded, coldly.

"That boy is in the way," she said to herself, when she was left alone. "He is in my way, and Tom's way. I can see that he is artfully intriguing for Mr. Wharton's favor, but I must checkmate him. It's odd," she resumed, after a pause, "but there is something in his face and voice that seems familiar to me. What is it?"

The following evening the housekeeper received another visit from her nephew.

"How do, aunt?" said Thomas Bradley, carelessly, as he entered the housekeeper's room.

"Very well, thank you, Thomas. I am glad you are here. I have been wanting to see you."

"The old man isn't going to do anything for me, is he?"

"How can you expect it so soon? He doesn't know you yet. How much do you think he pays the cash-boy that reads to him in the evening?"

"I don't know."

"Five dollars a week."

"I wouldn't give up my evenings for that," he said.

"It isn't so much the pay, Thomas, though that would be a help. He might take a fancy to you."

"That might pay better. When are you going to introduce me?"

"This evening; that is, I will ask Mr. Wharton if he will see you."

Mrs. Bradley entered the library, where Frank was engaged in reading aloud.

"Excuse my interruption," she said; "but my nephew has just called, and I should like to introduce him to you, if you will kindly receive him."

"Certainly, Mrs. Bradley," said Mr. Wharton. "Bring him in."

The housekeeper left the room, but speedily reappeared, followed by her nephew, who seemed a little abashed.

"My nephew, Thomas Bradley, Mr. Wharton," said his aunt, by way of introduction. "You have often heard me speak of Mr. Wharton, Thomas."

"How do you do, sir?" said Thomas awkwardly.

"Pray take a seat, Mr. Bradley. Your aunt has been long a member of my family. I am glad to see a nephew of hers. I believe you are a salesman at Gilbert & Mack's?"

"Yes, sir."

"Then you must know my young friend here?" pointing to Frank.

"How are you, Cash?" said Thomas, laughing, under the impression that he had said something smart.

"Very well, Mr. Bradley," answered Frank, quietly.

"You see, that's all the name we call 'em in the store," said Thomas.

Mr. Wharton could not help thinking:

"How poorly this young man compares with my young friend. Still, as he is Mrs. Bradley's nephew, I must be polite to him."

"Are there many cash-boys in your establishment, Mr. Bradley?"

"About a dozen. Ain't there, Fowler?"

"I believe so, Mr. Bradley."

"Gilbert & Mack do a good business, I should judge."

"Yes, they do; but that doesn't do us poor salesmen much good. We get just enough to keep soul and body together."

"I am sorry to hear it," said Mr. Wharton.

"Why, sir," said Thomas, gaining confidence, "all they pay me is twelve dollars a week. How can they expect a fellow to live on that?"

"I began my career about your age," said Mr. Wharton, "or perhaps a little younger, and had to live on but six dollars a week."

"Didn't you come near starving?" he asked.

"On the contrary, I saved a little every week."

"I can't," said Thomas, a little discomfited. "Why, it takes half that to dress decently."

Mr. Wharton glanced quietly at the rather loud and flashy dress worn by his visitor, but only said:

"A small salary, of course, makes economy necessary."

"But when a fellow knows he earns a good deal more than he gets, he doesn't feel like starving himself just that his employers may grow rich."

"Of course, if he can better himself they cannot object."

"That's just what I want to do," said Thomas; "but I expect I need influence to help me to something better. That's a good hint," thought he.

"I was telling Thomas," said the housekeeper, "that you had kindly expressed a desire to be of service to him."

"I am not now in active business," said Mr. Wharton, "and of course have not the opportunities I formerly had for helping young men, but I will bear your case in mind, Mr. Bradley."

"Thank you, sir," said Thomas. "I am sure I earn a thousand dollars a year."

"I think, Thomas," said Mrs. Bradley, "we won't intrude on Mr. Wharton longer this evening. When he finds something for you he will tell me."

"All right, aunt. Good-night, Mr. Wharton. Good-night, Cash," said Thomas, chuckling anew at the old joke.

"Well, aunt," said he, when they were once more in the housekeeper's room, "do you think the old gentleman will do anything for me?"

"I hope so; but I am not sure, Thomas, whether you were not too familiar. You spoke of money too quick."

"It's my way to come to business."

"I wish you were his reader, instead of that boy."

"Well, I don't. I wouldn't want to be mewed up in that room with the old man every night. I should get tired to death of it."

"You would have a chance to get him interested in you. That boy is artful; he is doing all he can to win Mr. Wharton's favor. He is the one you have most reason to dread."

"Do you think he will do me any harm?"

"I think he will injure your chances."

"Egad! if I thought that, I'd wring the young rascal's neck."

"There's a better way, Thomas."

"What's that?"

"Can't you get him dismissed from Gilbert & Mack's?"

"I haven't enough influence with the firm."

"Suppose they thought him dishonest?"

"They'd give him the sack, of course."

"Can't you make them think so, Thomas?"

"I don't know."

"Then make it your business to find out."

"I suppose you know what good it's going to do, aunt, but I don't. He's got his place here with the old man."

"If Mr. Wharton hears that he is discharged, and has lost his situation, he will probably discharge him, too."

"Perhaps so; I suppose you know best."

"Do as I tell you, and I will manage the rest."

"All right. I need your help enough. To-night, for instance, I'm regularly cleaned out. Haven't got but twenty-five cents to my name."

"It seems to me, Thomas," said his aunt, with a troubled look, "you are always out of money. I'll give you five dollars, Thomas, but you must remember that I am not made of money. My wages are small."

"You ought to have a good nest-egg laid aside, aunt."

"I've got something, Thomas, and when I die, it'll be yours."

"I hope I shan't have to wait too long," thought Thomas, "but he did not give utterance to the thought."

"Come again, Thomas, and don't forget what I have said," said Mrs. Bradley.

Chapter-XI
John Wade

A tall man, with a sallow complexion, and heavily-bearded face, stood on the deck of a Cunard steamer, only a few miles distant from New York harbor.

"It's three years since I have seen America," he said to himself, thoughtfully. "I suppose I ought to feel a patriotic fervor about setting foot once more on my native shore, but I don't believe in nonsense. I would be content to live in Europe all my life, if my uncle's fortune were once in my possession. I am his sole heir, but he persists in holding on to his money bags, and limits me to a paltry three thousand a year. I must see if I can't induce him to give me a good, round sum on account—fifty thousand, at least—and then I can wait a little more patiently till he drops off."

"When shall we reach port, captain?" he asked, as he passed that officer.

"In four hours, I think, Mr. Wade."

"So this is my birthday," he said to himself.

"Thirty five years old to-day. Half my life gone, and I am still a dependent on my uncle's bounty. Suppose he should throw me off—leave me out in the cold—where should I be? If he should find the boy—but no, there is no chance of that. I have taken good care of that. By the way, I must look him up soon—cautiously, of course—and see what has become of him. He will grow up a laborer or mechanic and die without a knowledge of his birth, while I fill his place and enjoy his inheritance."

At six o'clock the vessel reached the Quarantine. Most of the passengers decided to remain on board one night more, but John Wade was impatient, and, leaving his trunks, obtained a small boat, and soon touched the shore.

It was nearly eight when John Wade landed in the city. It was half-past eight when he stood on the steps of his uncle's residence and rang the bell.

"Is my uncle is Mr. Wharton—at home?" he asked of the servant who answered the bell.

"Yes, sir."

"I am his nephew, just arrived from Europe. Let him know that I am here, and would like to see him."

The servant, who had never before seen him, having only been six months in the house, regarded him with a great deal of curiosity, and then went to do his biding.

"My nephew arrived!" exclaimed Mr. Wharton, in surprise. "Why, he never let me know he was coming."

"Will you see him, sir?"

"To be sure! Bring him in at once."

"My dear uncle!" exclaimed John Wade, with effusion, for he was a polite man, and could act when it suited his interests to do so, "I am glad to see you. How is your health?"

"I am getting older every day, John."

"You don't look a day older, sir," said John, who did not believe what he said, for he could plainly see that his uncle had grown older since he last saw him.

"You think so, John, but I feel it. Your coming is a surprise. You did not write that you intended sailing."

"I formed the determination very suddenly, sir."

"Were you tired of Europe?"

"No; but I wanted to see you, sir."

"Thank you, John," said his uncle, pressing his nephew's hand. "I am glad you think so much of me. Did you have a pleasant voyage?"

"Rather rough, sir."

"You have had no supper, of course? If you will ring the bell, the housekeeper will see that some is got ready for you."

"Is Mrs. Bradley still in your employ, uncle?"

"Yes, John. I am so used to her that I shouldn't know how to get along without her."

Hitherto John Wade had been so occupied with his uncle that he had not observed Frank. But at this moment our hero coughed, involuntarily, and John Wade looked at him. He seemed to be singularly affected. He started perceptibly, and his sallow face blanched, as his eager eyes were fixed on the boy's face.

"Good heavens!" he muttered to himself. "Who is that boy? How comes he here?"

Frank noticed his intent gaze, and wondered at it, but Mr. Wharton's eyesight was defective, and he did not perceive his nephew's excitement.

"I see you have a young visitor, uncle," said John Wade.

"Oh, yes," said Mr. Wharton, with a kindly smile. "He spends all his evenings with me."

"What do you mean, sir?" demanded John Wade, with sudden suspicion and fear. "He seems very young company for— —"

"For a man of my years," said Mr. Wharton, finishing the sentence. "You are right, John. But, you see, my eyes are weak, and I cannot use them for reading in the evening, so it occurred to me to engage a reader."

"Very true," said his nephew. He wished to inquire the name of the boy whose appearance had so powerfully impressed him but he determined not to do so at present. What information he sought he preferred to obtain from the housekeeper.

"He seemed surprised, as if he had seen me some where before, and recognized me," thought Frank, "but I don't remember him. If I had seen his face before, I think I should remember it."

"Don't come out, uncle." said John Wade, when summoned to tea by the housekeeper. "Mrs. Bradley and I are going to have a chat by ourselves, and I will soon return."

"You are looking thin, Mr. John," said Mrs Bradley.

"Am I thinner than usual? I never was very corpulent, you know. How is my uncle's health? He says he is well."

"He is pretty well, but he isn't as young as he was."

"I think he looks older," said John. "But that is not surprising—at his age. He is seventy, isn't he?"

"Not quite. He is sixty-nine."

"His father died at seventy-one."

"Yes."

"But that is no reason why my uncle should not live till eighty. I hope he will."

"We all hope so," said the housekeeper; but she knew, while she spoke, that if, as she supposed, Mr. Wharton's will contained a generous legacy for her, his death would not afflict her much. She suspected also that John Wade was waiting impatiently for his uncle's death, that he might enter upon his inheritance. Still, their little social fictions must be kept up, and so both expressed a desire for his continued life, though neither was deceived as to the other's real feeling on the subject.

"By the way, Mrs. Bradley," said John Wade, "how came my uncle to engage that boy to read to him?"

"He was led into it, sir," said the housekeeper, with a great deal of indignation, "by the boy himself. He's an artful and designing fellow, you may rely upon it."

"What's his name?"

"Frank Fowler."

"Fowler! Is his name Fowler?" he repeated, with a startled expression.

"Yes, sir," answered the housekeeper, rather surprised at his manner. "You don't know anything about him, do you?"

"Oh, no," said John Wade, recovering his composure. "He is a perfect stranger to me; but I once knew a man of that name, and a precious rascal he was. When you mentioned his name, I thought he might be a son of this man. Does he say his father is alive?"

"No; he is dead, and his mother, too, so the boy says."

"You haven't told me how my uncle fell in with him?"

"It was an accident. Your uncle fell in getting out of a Broadway stage, and this boy happened to be near, and seeing Mr. Wharton was a rich gentleman, he helped him home, and was invited in. Then he told some story about his poverty, and so worked upon your uncle's feelings that he hired him to read to him at five dollars a week."

"Is this all the boy does?"

"No; he is cash-boy in a large store on Broadway. He is employed there all day, and he is here only in the evenings."

"Does my uncle seem attached to him?" asked John.

"He's getting fond of him, I should say. The other day he asked me if I didn't think it would be a good thing to take him into the house and give him a room. I suppose the boy put it into his head."

"No doubt. What did you say?"

"I opposed it. I told him that a boy would be a great deal of trouble in the family."

"You did right, Mrs. Bradley. What did my uncle say?"

"He hinted about taking him from the store and letting him go to school. The next thing would be his adopting him. The fact is,

Mr. John, the boy is so artful that he knows just how to manage your uncle. No doubt he put the idea into Mr. Wharton's head, and he may do it yet."

"Does my uncle give any reason for the fancy he has taken to the boy?" demanded John.

"Yes," said the housekeeper. "He has taken it into his head that the boy resembles your cousin, George, who died abroad. You were with him, I believe?"

"Yes, I was with him. Is the resemblance strong? I took very little notice of him."

"You can look for yourself when you go back," answered the housekeeper.

"What else did my uncle say? Tell me all."

"He said: 'What would I give, Mrs. Bradley, if I had such a grandson? If George's boy had lived, he would have been about Frank's age. And," continued the housekeeper, "I might as well speak plainly. You're my master's heir, or ought to be; but if this artful boy stays here long, there's no knowing what your uncle may be influenced to do. If he gets into his dotage, he may come to adopt him, and leave the property away from you."

"I believe you are quite right. The danger exists, and we must guard against it. I see you don't like the boy," said John Wade.

"No, I don't. He's separated your uncle and me. Before he came, I used to spend my evenings in the library, and read to your uncle. Besides, when I found your uncle wanted a reader, I asked him to take my nephew, who is a salesman in the very same store where that boy is a cash-boy, but although I've been twenty years in this house I could not get him to grant the favor, which he granted to that boy, whom he never met till a few weeks ago."

"Mrs. Bradley, I sympathize with you," said her companion. "The boy is evidently working against us both. You have been twenty years in my uncle's service. He ought to remember you handsomely in his will. If I inherit the property, as is my right, your services shall be remembered," said John Wade.

"Thank you, Mr. John," said the gratified housekeeper.

"That secures her help," thought John, in his turn.

"She will now work hard for me. When the time comes, I can do as much or as little for her as I please."

"Of course, we must work together against this interloper, who appears to have gained a dangerous influence over my uncle."

"You can depend upon me, Mr. John," said Mrs. Bradley.

"I will think it over, and tell you my plan," said John Wade. "But my uncle will wonder at my appetite. I must go back to the library. We will speak of this subject again."

Chapter-XII

A False Friend

When John Wade re-entered the library, Frank was reading, but Mr. Wharton stopped him.

"That will do, Frank," he said. "As I have not seen my nephew for a long time, I shall not require you to read any longer. You can go, if you like."

Frank bowed, and bidding the two good-evening, left the room.

"That is an excellent boy, John." said the old gentleman, as the door closed upon our hero.

"How did you fall in with him?" asked John. Mr. Wharton told the story with which the reader is already familiar.

"You don't know anything of his antecedents, I suppose?" said John, carelessly.

"Only what he told me. His father and mother are dead, and he is obliged to support himself and his sister. Did you notice anything familiar in Frank's expression?" asked Mr. Wharton.

"I don't know. I didn't observe him very closely."

"Whenever I look at Frank, I think of George. I suppose that is why I have felt more closely drawn to the boy. I proposed to Mrs. Bradley that the boy should have a room here, but she did not favor it. I think she is prejudiced against him."

"Probably she is afraid he would be some trouble," replied John.

"If George's boy had lived he would be about Frank's age. It would have been a great comfort to me to superintend his education, and watch him grow up. I could not have wished him to be more gentlemanly or promising than my young reader."

"Decidedly, that boy is in my way," said John Wade to himself. "I must manage to get rid of him, and that speedily, or my infatuated uncle will be adopting him."

"Of what disease did George's boy die, John?" asked Mr. Wharton.

"A sudden fever."

"I wish I could have seen him before he died. But I returned only to find both son and grandson gone. I had only the sad satisfaction of seeing his grave."

"Yes, he was buried in the family lot at Greenwood, five days before you reached home."

"When I see men of my own age, surrounded by children and grandchildren, it makes me almost envious," said Mr. Wharton, sadly. "I declare to you, John, since that boy has been with me, I have felt happier and more cheerful than for years."

"That boy again!" muttered John to himself. "I begin to hate the young cub, but I mustn't show it. My first work will be to separate him from my uncle. That will require consideration. I wonder whether the boy knows that he is not Fowler's son? I must find out. If he does, and should happen to mention it in my uncle's presence, it might awaken suspicions in his mind. I must interview the boy, and find out what I can. To enlist his confidence, I must assume a friendly manner."

In furtherance of this determination, John Wade greeted our hero very cordially the next evening, when they met, a little to Frank's surprise.

When the reading terminated, John Wade said, carelessly:

"I believe, uncle, I will go out for a walk. I think I shall be better for it. In what direction are you going, Frank?"

"Down Sixth Avenue, sir."

"Very good; I will walk along with you."

Frank and his companion walked toward Sixth Avenue.

"My uncle tells me you have a sister to support," said Wade, opening the conversation.

"Yes, sir."

"Does your sister resemble you?" asked John Wade.

"No, sir! but that is not surprising, for— —"

"Why is it not surprising?"

Frank hesitated.

"You were about to assign some reason."

"It is a secret," said our hero, slowly; "that is, has been a secret, but I don't know why I should conceal it. Grace is not my sister. She is Mrs. Fowler's daughter, but I am not her son. I will tell you the story."

That story Frank told as briefly as possible. John Wade listened to it with secret alarm.

"It is a strange story," he said. "Do you not feel a strong desire to learn your true parentage?"

"Yes, sir. I don't know, but I feel as if I should some day meet the man who gave me into Mrs. Fowler's charge."

"You have met him, but it is lucky you don't suspect it," thought John Wade.

"I am glad you told me this story," said he, aloud.

"It is quite romantic. I may be able to help you in your search. But let me advise you to tell no one else at present. No doubt there are parties interested in keeping the secret of your birth from you. You must move cautiously, and your chance of solving the mystery will be improved."

"Thank you, sir. I will follow your advice."

"I was mistaken in him," thought Frank. "I disliked him at first, but he seems inclined to be my friend."

When Frank reached his lodging he found Jasper waiting up for him. He looked thoughtful, so much so that Frank noticed it.

"You look as if you had something on your mind," Jasper.

"You have guessed right. I have read that letter."

He drew from his pocket a letter, which Frank took from his hands.

"It is from an uncle of mine in Ohio, who is proprietor of a weekly newspaper. He is getting old, and finds the work too much for him. He offers me a thousand dollars a year if I will come out and relieve him."

"That's a good offer, Jasper. I suppose you will accept it?"

"It is for my interest to do so. Probably my uncle will, after a while, surrender the whole establishment to me."

"I shall be sorry to part with you, Jasper. It will seem very lonely, but I think you ought to go. It is a good chance, and if you refuse it you may not get such another."

"My uncle wants me to come on at once. I think I will start Monday."

Jasper saw no reason to change his determination, and on Monday morning he started on his journey to Ohio.

Thus, at a critical moment in his fortunes, when two persons were planning to injure him, he lost the presence and help of a valued friend.

Chapter-XIII

The Spider and the Fly

Uncle," said John Wade, "you spoke of inviting Frank Fowler to occupy a room in the house. Why don't you do it? It would be more convenient to you and a very good chance for him."

"I should like it," said Mr. Wharton, "but Mrs. Bradley did not seem to regard it favorably when I suggested it."

"Oh, Mrs. Bradley is unused to boys, and she is afraid he would give her trouble. I'll undertake to bring her around."

"I wish you would, John. I don't think Frank would give any trouble, and it would enliven the house to have a boy here. Besides, he reminds me of George, as I told you the other day."

"I agree with you, uncle," he said. "He does remind me a little of George."

"Well, Mrs. Bradley, what do you think I have done?" asked John, entering the housekeeper's room directly after his interview with his uncle.

"I don't know, Mr. John," she answered.

"I have asked him to give that boy a room in the house."

"Are you carried away with him as well as your uncle?"

"Not quite. The fact is, I have a motive in what I am doing. I'll tell you."

He bent over and whispered in her ear.

"I never should have thought of that."

"You see, our purpose is to convince my uncle that he is unworthy of his favor. At present that would be rather difficult, but once get him into the house and we shall have no trouble."

"I understand."

In due time John Wade announced to his uncle that the housekeeper had withdrawn her objections to his plan.

"Then I'll tell him to-night," said Mr. Wharton, brightening up.

Shortly after Frank entered the library that evening Mr. Wharton made the proposal.

"You are very kind, Mr. Wharton," he said. "I never thought of such a thing."

"Then it is settled that you are to come. You can choose your own time for coming."

"I will come to-morrow, sir."

"Very well," said Mr. Wharton, with satisfaction.

The next day, by special favor, Frank got off from the store two hours earlier than usual. He bought at a Sixth Avenue basement store, a small, second hand trunk for two dollars. He packed his scanty wardrobe into the trunk, which, small as it was he was unable to fill, and had it carried to Mr. Wharton's house.

He asked to see Mrs. Bradley, and she came to the door.

"I am glad to see you," she said graciously. "You may leave your trunk in the hall and I will have it carried up by the servants."

"Thank you," said Frank, and he followed the housekeeper up the handsome staircase.

"This is to be your room," said the housekeeper, opening the door of a small chamber on the third floor.

"It looks very nice and comfortable," said Frank, looking about him with satisfaction.

She left the room, and five minutes later our hero's modest trunk was brought up and deposited in the room.

That evening Frank read to Mr. Wharton as usual.

When nine o'clock came he said:

"You need not read aloud any more, but if you see any books in my library which you would like to read to yourself you may do so. In fact, Frank, you must consider yourself one of the family, and act as freely as if you were at home."

"How kind you are to me, Mr. Wharton," said Frank.

The next morning after Frank had left the house for his daily task, John Wade entered the housekeeper's room.

"The boy is out of the way now, Mrs. Bradley," he said. "You had better see if you have a key that will unlock his trunk."

The two conspirators went upstairs, and together entered Frank's room.

Mrs. Bradley brought out a large bunch of keys, and successively tried them, but one after another failed to open it.

"That's awkward," said John Wade. "I have a few keys in my pocket. One may possibly answer."

The housekeeper kneeled down, and made a trial of John Wade's keys. The last one was successful. The cover was lifted, and the contents were disclosed. However, neither John nor Mrs. Bradley seemed particularly interested in the articles for after turning them over they locked the trunk once more.

"So far so good," said John Wade. "We have found the means of opening the trunk when we please."

"When do you expect to carry out your plan, Mr. John?"

"Two weeks from this time my uncle is obliged to go to Washington for a few days on business. While he is gone we will spring the trap, and when he comes back he will find the boy gone in disgrace. We'll make short work of him."

Chapter-XIV
Springing the Trap

I am going to give you a few days' vacation, Frank," said Mr. Wharton, a fortnight later. "I am called to Washington on business. However, you have got to feel at home here now."

"Oh, yes, sir."

"And Mrs. Bradley will see that you are comfortable."

"I am sure of that, sir," said Frank, politely.

When Frank returned at night, Mr. Wharton was already gone. John Wade and the housekeeper seated themselves in the library after dinner, and by their invitation our hero joined them.

"By the way, Frank," said John Wade, "did I ever show you this Russia leather pocketbook?" producing one from his pocket.

"No, sir, I believe not."

"I bought it at Vienna, which is noted for its articles of Russia leather."

"It is very handsome, sir."

"So I think. By the way, you may like to look at my sleeve-buttons. They are of Venetian mosaic. I got them myself in Venice last year."

"They are very elegant. You must have enjoyed visiting so many famous cities."

"Yes; it is very interesting."

John Wade took up the evening paper, and Frank occupied himself with a book from his patron's library. After a while John threw down the paper yawning, and said that he had an engagement. Nothing else occurred that evening which merits record.

Two days later Frank returned home in his usual spirits. But at the table he was struck by a singular change in the manner of Mrs. Bradley and John Wade. They spoke to him only on what it was absolutely necessary, and answered his questions in monosyllables.

"Will you step into the library a moment?" said John Wade, as they arose from the table.

Frank followed John into the library, and Mrs. Bradley entered also.

"Frank Fowler," the enemy began, "do you remember my showing you two evenings since a pocketbook, also some sleeve-buttons of Venetian mosaic, expensively mounted in gold?"

"Certainly, sir."

"That pocketbook contained a considerable sum of money," pursued his questioner.

"I don't know anything about that."

"You probably supposed so."

"Will you tell me what you mean, Mr. Wade?" demanded Frank, impatiently. "I have answered your questions, but I can't understand why you ask them."

"Perhaps you may suspect," said Wade, sarcastically.

"It looks as if you had lost them and suspected me of taking them."

"So it appears."

"You are entirely mistaken, Mr. Wade. I am not a thief. I never stole anything in my life."

"It is very easy to say that," sneered John Wade. "You and Mrs. Bradley were the only persons present when I showed the articles, and I suppose you won't pretend that she stole them?"

"No, sir; though she appears to agree with you that I am a thief. I never thought of accusing her," replied Frank.

"Mr. Wade," said the housekeeper, "I feel that it is my duty to insist upon search being made in my room."

"Do you make the same offer?" asked John Wade, turning to Frank.

"Yes, sir," answered our hero, proudly. "I wish you to satisfy yourself that I am not a thief. If you will come to my room at once, Mr. Wade, you and Mrs. Bradley, I will hand you the key of my trunk."

The two followed him upstairs, exulting wickedly in his discomfiture, which they had reason to forsee.

He handed his key to his artful enemy, and the latter bending over, opened the trunk, which contained all our hero's small possessions.

He raised the pile of clothes, and, to Frank's dismay, disclosed the missing pocketbook and sleeve-buttons in the bottom of the trunk.

"What have you got to say for yourself now, you young villain?" demanded John Wade, in a loud voice.

"I don't understand it," Frank said, in a troubled tone. "I don't know how the things came there. I didn't put them there."

"Probably they crept in themselves," sneered John.

"Someone put them there," said Frank, pale, but resolute; "some wicked person, who wanted to get me into trouble."

"What do you mean by that, you young vagabond?" demanded John Wade, suspiciously.

"I mean what I say," he asserted. "I am away all day, and nothing is easier than to open my trunk and put articles in, in order to throw suspicion on me."

"Look here, you rascal!" said John Wade, roughly. "I shall treat you better than you deserve. I won't give you over to the police out of regard for my uncle, but you must leave this house and never set foot in it again. It will be the worse for you if you do."

John Wade and the housekeeper left the room, and our hero was left to realize the misfortune which had overwhelmed him.

Frank arose at an early hour the next morning and left the house. It was necessary for him to find a new home at once in order to be at the store in time. He bought a copy of the Sun and turned to the advertising columns. He saw a cheap room advertised near the one he had formerly occupied. Finding his way there he rang the bell.

The door was opened by a slatternly-looking woman, who looked as if she had just got up.

"I see by the Sun you have a room to let," said Frank.

"Yes; do you want to see it now?"

"I should like to."

"Come upstairs and I will show you the room."

The room proved to be small, and by no means neat in appearance, but the rent was only a dollar and a quarter a week, and Frank felt that he could not afford to be particular, so he quickly closed the bargain.

The next day, about eleven o'clock in the forenoon, he was surprised at seeing Mrs. Bradley enter the store and thread her way to that part of the counter where her nephew was stationed. She darted one quick look at him, but gave him no sign of recognition. His heart sank within him, for he had a presentiment that her visit boded fresh evil for him.

❖❖❖

Chapter-XV
From Bad to Worse

Frank's misgivings were not without good cause. The housekeeper's call at the store was connected with him. How, will be understood from a conversation which took place that morning between her and John Wade.

"It's a relief to get that boy out of the house, Mrs. Bradley," he said at the breakfast table.

"That it is, Mr. John," she replied. "But he'll be trying to get back, take my word for it."

"He won't dare to," said John Wade, incredulously. "I told him if he came near the house I would give him up to the police."

"I am afraid he will write to your uncle. He's bold enough for anything."

"I didn't think of that," said John, thoughtfully.

"Do you know his handwriting, Mrs. Bradley?"

"I think I should know it."

"Then if any letters come which you know to be from him, keep them back from my uncle."

"What shall I do with them?"

"Give them to me. I don't want my uncle worried by his appeals."

"Your uncle seems to be very attached to him. He may go to the store to see him."

"That is true. I should not like that. How shall we prevent it, that's the question."

"If Gilbert & Mack knew that he was not honest they would discharge him."

"Exactly," said John Wade; "and as probably he would be unable to get another situation, he would be compelled to leave the city, and we should get rid of him. I commend your shrewdness, Mrs. Bradley. Your plan is most excellent."

John Wade had more reasons than the housekeeper knew of for desiring the removal of our young hero from the city—reasons which the reader has probably guessed. There was a dark secret in his life connected with a wrong done in years past, from which he hoped some day to reap personal benefit. Unconsciously Frank Fowler stood in his way, and must be removed. Such was his determination.

"I am going out this morning," said the housekeeper. "I will make it in my way to call at Gilbert & Mack's. My nephew is a salesman there, as I have told you. I will drop a word in his ear, and that will be enough to settle that boy's hash."

"Your language is professional, Mrs. Bradley," said John Wade, laughing, "but you shouldn't allude to hash in an aristocratic household. I shall be glad to have you carry out your plan."

"I hope you'll speak to your uncle about my nephew, Mr. John. He gets very poor pay where he is."

"I won't forget him," said John, carelessly.

In his heart he thought Thomas Bradley a very low, obtrusive fellow, whom he felt by no means inclined to assist, but it was cheap to make promises.

The reader understands now why Mrs. Bradley made a morning call at Gilbert & Mack's store.

She knew at what part of the counter her nephew was stationed, and made her way thither at once. He did not at first recognize her, until she said:

"Good-morning, Thomas."

"Good-morning, aunt. What brings you here this morning? Any good news for me? Has the old gentleman come around and concluded to do something handsome?"

"Mr. Wharton is not in the city. He has gone to Washington. But that isn't what I came about this morning. You remember that boy who has been reading to Mr. Wharton?"

"One of our cash-boys. Yes; there he is, just gone by."

"Well, he has stolen Mr. John's pocketbook and some jewelry belonging to him."

"What have you done about it? What does Mr. Wharton say?"

"He's away from home. He doesn't know yet. Mr. John gave him a lecture, and ordered him to leave the house."

"Does he admit that he took the things?"

"No; he denied it as bold as brass, but it didn't do him any good. There were the things in his trunk. He couldn't get over that."

Thomas fastened a shrewd glance on his aunt's face, for he suspected the truth.

"So you've got rid of him?" he said. "What do you propose to do next?"

"Mr. John thinks your employer ought to know that he is a thief."

"Are you going to tell them?"

"I want you to do it."

"You must tell them yourself, aunt. I shan't."

"Then introduce me to Mr. Gilbert, Thomas, and I'll do it."

"Follow me, aunt."

He led his aunt to the rear of the store, where Mr. Gilbert was standing.

"Mr. Gilbert," he said, "allow me to introduce my aunt, Mrs. Bradley."

The housekeeper was courteously received, and invited to be seated. She soon opened her business, and blackened poor Frank's character as she had intended.

"Really, Mrs. Bradley, I am sorry to hear this," said Mr. Gilbert. "You think there is no doubt of the boy's guilt?"

"I am sorry to say that I have no doubt at all," said the housekeeper, hypocritically.

"Mr. Mack and myself have had a very good opinion of him. He is faithful and prompt."

"Of course, sir, you will retain him in your employ if you are willing to take the risk, but I thought it my duty to put you on your guard."

"I am obliged to you, Mrs. Bradley; though, as I said, I regret to find that my confidence in the boy has been misplaced."

Late in the afternoon, Frank was called to the cashier's desk.

"I am directed by Mr. Gilbert to say that your services will not be required after to-day," he said. "Here are the week's wages."

"Why am I discharged? What have I done?" demanded Frank, while his heart sank within him.

"I don't know. You must ask Mr. Gilbert," answered the cashier.

"I will speak to him, at any rate," and Frank walked up to the senior partner, and addressed to him the same question.

"Can you not guess?" asked Mr. Gilbert, sternly.

"I can guess that a false accusation has been brought against me," said Frank.

"A respectable lady has informed me that you are not honest. I regret it, for I have been pleased with your diligence. Of course, I cannot retain you in my employ."

"Mr. Gilbert," said Frank, earnestly, "the charge is false. Mrs. Bradley is my enemy, and wishes me harm. I don't understand how the things came into my trunk, but I didn't put them there."

"I hope you are innocent, but I must discharge you. Business is dull now, and I had decided to part with four of my cash-boys. I won't pass judgment upon you, but you must go."

Frank bowed in silence, for he saw that further entreaty would be vain, and left the store more dispirited than at any moment since he had been in the city.

Ten days Frank spent in fruitless efforts to obtain a place.

All this time his money steadily diminished. He perceived that he would soon be penniless. Evidently, something must be done. He formed two determinations. The first was to write to Mr. Wharton, who, he thought, must now have returned from Washington, asserting his innocence and appealing to him to see Gilbert & Mack, and re-establish him in their confidence. The second was, since he could not obtain a regular place, to frequent the wharves and seek chances to carry bundles. In this way he might earn enough, with great economy, to pay for his board and lodging.

One morning the housekeeper entered the library where John Wade sat reading the daily papers.

"Mr. John," she said, holding out a letter, "here is a letter from that boy. I expected he would write to your uncle."

John Wade deliberately opened the letter.

"Sit down, Mrs. Bradley, and I will read the letter aloud."

It will be only necessary to quote the concluding sentences:

"'I hope, Mr. Wharton, you will not be influenced against me by what Mrs. Bradley and your nephew say. I don't know why it is, but they are my enemies, though I have always treated them with respect. I am afraid they have a desire to injure me in your estimation. If they had not been, they would have been content with driving me from your house, without also slandering me to my employers, and inducing them to discharge me. Since I was discharged, I have tried very hard to get another place, but as I cannot bring a recommendation from Gilbert & Mack, I have everywhere been refused. I ask you, Mr. Wharton to consider my situation. Already my small supply of money is nearly gone, and I do not know how I am to pay my expenses. If it was any fault of mine that had brought me into this situation, I would not complain, but it seems hard to suffer when I am innocent.

"'I do not ask to return to your house, Mr. Wharton, for it would not be pleasant, since your nephew and Mrs. Bradley dislike me, but I have a right to ask that the truth may be told to my employers, so that if they do not wish me to return to their service, they may, at least, be willing to give me a recommendation that will give me a place elsewhere."'

"I must prevent the boy communicating with my uncle, if it is a possible thing. 'Strike while the iron is hot,' I say."

"I think that is very judicious, Mr. John. I have no doubt you will know how to manage matters."

John Wade dressed himself for a walk, and drawing out a cigar, descended the steps of his uncle's house into the street.

He reached Fifth Avenue, and walked slowly downtown. He was about opposite Twenty-eighth Street, when he came face to face with the subject of his thoughts.

"Where are you going?" John Wade demanded sternly.

"I don't know that I am bound to answer your question," answered Frank, quietly, "but I have no objection. I am going to Thirty-ninth Street with this bundle."

"Hark you, boy! I have something to say to you," continued John Wade, harshly. "You have had the impudence to write to my uncle."

"What did he say?"

"Nothing that you would like to hear. He looks upon you as a thief."

"You have slandered me to him, Mr. Wade," he said, angrily. "You might be in better business than accusingly a poor boy falsely."

"Hark you, young man! I have had enough of your impudence. I will give you a bit of advice, which you will do well to follow. Leave this city for a place where you are not known, or I may feel disposed to shut you up on a charge of theft."

"I shall not leave the city, Mr. Wade," returned Frank, firmly. "I shall stay here in spite of you," and without waiting for an answer, he walked on.

Chapter-XVI

An Accomplice Found

No sooner had John Wade parted from our hero than he saw approaching him a dark, sinister-looking man, whom he had known years before.

"Good-morning, Mr. Wade," said the newcomer.

"Good-morning, Mr. Graves. Are you busy just now?"

"No, sir; I am out of employment. I have been unfortunate."

"Then I will give you a job. Do you see that boy?" said John Wade, rapidly.

"Yes, I see him."

"I want you to follow him. Find out where he lives, and let me know this evening. Do you understand?"

"I understand. You may rely upon me, sir," answered Nathan Graves; and quickening his pace, he soon came within a hundred feet of our hero.

After fulfilling his errand, Frank walked downtown again, but did not succeed in obtaining any further employment. Wherever he went, he was followed by Graves. Unconsciously, he exhausted the patience of that gentleman, who got heartily tired of his tramp about the streets. But the longest day will come to an end, and at last he had the satisfaction of tracking Frank to his humble lodging. Then, and not till then, he felt justified in leaving him.

Nathan Graves sought the residence of John Wade. He rang the bell as the clock struck eight.

"Well, what success?" asked Wade, when they met.

"I have tracked the boy. What more can I do for you?" asked Graves.

"I want to get him away from the city. The fact is—I may as well tell you—my uncle has taken a great fancy to the boy, and might be induced to adopt him, and cut me off from my rightful inheritance. The boy is an artful young rascal, and has been doing all he could to get into the good graces of my uncle, who is old and weak-minded."

It was nine o'clock when Nathan Graves left the house, John Wade himself accompanying him to the door.

"How soon do you think you can carry out my instructions?" asked Wade.

"To-morrow, if possible."

"The sooner the better."

"It is lucky I fell in with him," said Nathan Graves to himself, with satisfaction, as he slowly walked down Fifth Avenue. "It's a queer business, but that's none of my business. The main thing for me to consider is that it brings money to my purse, and of that I have need enough."

Graves left the house richer by a hundred dollars than he entered it.

It was eleven o'clock on the forenoon of the next day when Frank walked up Canal Street toward Broadway. He had been down to the wharves since early in the morning, seeking for employment. He had offered his services to many, but as yet had been unable to secure a job.

As he was walking along a man addressed him:

"Will you be kind enough to direct me to Broadway?"

It was Nathan Graves, with whom Frank was destined to have some unpleasant experiences.

"Straight ahead," answered Frank. "I am going there, and will show you, if you like."

"Thank you, I wish you would. I live only fifteen or twenty miles distant," said Graves, "but I don't often come to the city, and am not much acquainted. I keep a dry-goods store, but my partner generally comes here to buy goods. By the way, perhaps you can help me about the errand that calls me here today."

"I will, sir, if I can," said Frank, politely.

"My youngest clerk has just left me, and I want to find a successor—a boy about your age, say. Do you know any one who would like such a position?"

"I am out of employment myself just now. Do you think I will suit?"

"I think you will," said Mr. Graves.

"You won't object to go into the country?"

"No, sir."

"I will give you five dollars a week and your board for the present. If you suit me, your pay will be raised at the end of six months. Will that be satisfactory?" asked his companion.

"Quite so, sir. When do you wish me to come?"

"Can you go out with me this afternoon?"

"Yes, sir. I only want to go home and pack up my trunk."

"To save time, I will go with you, and we will start as soon as possible."

Nathan Graves accompanied Frank to his room, where his scanty wardrobe was soon packed. A hack was called, and they were speedily on their way to the Cortland Street ferry.

They crossed the ferry, and Mr. Graves purchased two tickets to Elizabeth. He bought a paper, and occupied himself in reading. Frank felt that fortune had begun to shine upon him once more. By and by, he could send for Grace, and get her boarded near him. As soon as his wages were raised, he determined to do this. While engaged in these pleasant speculations, they reached the station.

"We get out here," said Mr. Graves.

"Is your store in this place?" asked Frank.

"No; it is in the next town."

Nathan Graves looked about him for a conveyance. He finally drove a bargain with a man driving a shabby-looking vehicle, and the two took their seats.

They were driven about six miles through a flat, unpicturesque country, when they reached a branch road leading away from the main one.

It was a narrow road, and apparently not much frequented. Frank could see no houses on either side.

"Is your store on this road?" he asked.

"Oh, no; but I am not going to the store yet. We will go to my house, and leave your trunk."

At length the wagon stopped, by Graves' orders, in front of a gate hanging loosely by one hinge.

"We'll get out here," said Graves.

Frank looked with some curiosity, and some disappointment, at his future home. It was a square, unpainted house, discolored by time, and looked far from attractive. There were no outward signs of occupation, and everything about it appeared to have fallen into decay. Not far off was a barn, looking even more dilapidated than the house.

At the front door, instead of knocking—there was no bell—Graves drew a rusty key from his pocket and inserted it in the lock. They found themselves in a small entry, uncarpeted and dingy.

"We'll go upstairs," said Graves.

Arrived on the landing, he threw open a door, and ushered in our hero.

"This will be your room," he said.

Frank looked around in dismay.

It was a large, square room, uncarpeted, and containing only a bed, two chairs and a washstand, all of the cheapest and rudest manufacture.

"I hope you will soon feel at home here," said Graves. "I'll go down and see if I can find something to eat."

He went out, locking the door behind him

"What does this mean?" thought Frank, with a strange sensation.

❖❖❖

Chapter-XVII

Frank and his Jailer

It was twenty minutes before Frank, waiting impatiently, heard the steps of his late companion ascending the stairs.

But the door was not unlocked. Instead, a slide was revealed, about eight inches square, through which his late traveling companion pushed a plate of cold meat and bread.

"Here's something to eat," he said; "take it."

"Why do you lock me in?" demanded our hero.

"You can get along without knowing, I suppose," said the other, with a sneer.

"I don't mean to," said Frank, firmly. "I demand an explanation. How long do you intend to keep me here?"

"I am sorry I can't gratify your curiosity, but I don't know myself."

"Perhaps you think that I am rich, but I am not. I have no money. You can't get anything out of me," said Frank.

"That may be so, but I shall keep you."

"I suppose that was all a lie about your keeping store?"

"It was a pretty little story, told for your amusement, my dear boy," said Graves. "I was afraid you wouldn't come without it."

"You are a villain!" said Frank.

"Look here, boy," said Graves, in a different tone, his face darkening, "you had better not talk in that way. I advise you to eat your dinner and be quiet. Some supper will be brought to you before night."

So saying, he abruptly closed the slide, and descended the stairs, leaving Frank to his reflections, which it may be supposed, were not of the pleasantest character.

Frank did not allow his unpleasant situation to take away his appetite, and though he was fully determined to make the earliest possible attempt to escape, he was sensible enough first to eat the food which his jailer had brought him.

His lunch dispatched, he began at once to revolve plans of escape.

There were three windows in the room, two on the front of the house, the other at the side.

He tried one after another, but the result was the same. All were so fastened that it was quite impossible to raise them.

Feeling that he could probably escape through one of the windows when he pleased, though at the cost of considerable trouble, Frank did not trouble himself much, or allow himself to feel unhappy. He decided to continue his explorations.

In the corner of the room was a door, probably admitting to a closet.

"I suppose it is locked," thought Frank, but on trying it, he found that such was not the case. He looked curiously about him, but found little to repay him. His attention was drawn, however to several dark-colored masks lying upon a shelf.

He also discovered a small hole in the wall of the size of a marble. Actuated by curiosity, he applied his eye to the opening, and peeped into what was probably the adjoining room. It was furnished in very much the same way as the one in which he was confined, but at present it was untenanted. Having seen what little there was to be seen, Frank withdrew from his post of observation and returned to his room.

It was several hours later when he again heard steps ascending the stairs, and the slide in the door was moved.

He looked toward it, but the face that he saw was not that of Nathan Graves.

It was the face of a woman.

Chapter-XVIII

Over The Hill to The Poorhouse"

We are compelled for a time to leave our hero in the hands of his enemies, and return to the town of Crawford, where an event has occurred which influences seriously the happiness and position of his sister, Grace.

Ever since Frank left the town, Grace had been a welcome member of Mr. Pomeroy's family, receiving the kindest treatment from all, so that she had come to feel very much at home.

So they lived happily together, till one disastrous night a fire broke out, which consumed the house, and they were forced to snatch their clothes and escape, saving nothing else.

Mr. Pomeroy's house was insured for two-thirds of its value, and he proposed to rebuild immediately, but it would be three months at least before the new house would be completed. In the interim, he succeeded in hiring a couple of rooms for his family, but their narrow accommodations would oblige them to dispense with their boarder. Sorry as Mr. and Mrs. Pomeroy were to part with her, it was obvious that Grace must find another home.

"We must let Frank know," said Mr. Pomeroy, and having occasion to go up to the city at once to see about insurance, he went to the store of Gilbert & Mack, and inquired for Prank.

"Fowler? What was he?" was asked.

"A cash-boy."

"Oh, he is no longer here. Mr. Gilbert discharged him."

"Do you know why he was discharged?" asked Mr. Pomeroy, pained and startled.

"No; but there stands Mr. Gilbert. He can tell you."

Mr. Pomeroy introduced himself to the head of the firm and repeated his inquiry.

"If you are a friend of the lad," said Mr. Gilbert, "you will be sorry to learn that he was charged with dishonesty. It was a very respectable lady who made the charge. It is only fair to say that the boy denied it, and that, personally, we found him faithful and trusty. But as the dullness of trade compelled us to discharge some of our cash-boys, we naturally discharged him among the number, without, however, judging his case."

"Then, sir, you have treated the boy very unfairly. On the strength of a charge not proved, you have dismissed him, though personally you had noticed nothing out of the way in him, and rendered it impossible for him to obtain another place."

"There is something in what you say, I admit. Perhaps I was too hasty. If you will send the boy to me, I will take him back on probation."

"Thank you, sir," said Mr. Pomeroy, gratefully "I will send him here."

But this Mr. Pomeroy was unable to do. He did not know of Frank's new address, and though he was still in the city, he failed to find him.

He returned to Crawford and communicated the unsatisfactory intelligence. He tried to obtain a new boarding place for Grace, but no one was willing to take her at two dollars a week, especially when Mr. Pomeroy was compelled to admit that Frank was now out of employment, and it was doubtful if he would be able to keep up the payment.

Tom Pinkerton managed to learn that Grace was now without a home, and mentioned it to his father.

"Won't she have to go to the poorhouse now, father?" he asked eagerly.

"Yes," said Deacon Pinkerton. "There is no other place for her that I can see."

"Ah, I'm glad," said Tom, maliciously. "Won't that upstart's pride be taken down? He was too proud to go to the poorhouse, where he belonged, but he can't help his sister's going there. If he isn't a pauper himself, he'll be the brother of a pauper, and that's the next thing to it."

"That is true," said the deacon. "He was very impudent in return for my kindness. Still, I am sorry for him."

I am afraid the deacon's sorrow was not very deep, for he certainly looked unusually cheerful when he harnessed up his horse and drove around to the temporary home of the Pomeroys.

"Good-morning, Mr. Pomeroy," he said, seeing the latter in the yard. "You've met with a severe loss."

"Yes, deacon; it is a severe loss to a poor man like me."

"To be sure. Well, I've called around to relieve you of a part of your cares. I am going to take Grace Fowler to the poorhouse."

"Couldn't you get her a place with a private family to help about the house in return for her board, while she goes to school?"

"There's nobody wants a young girl like her," said the deacon.

"Her brother would pay part of her board—that is, when he has a place."

"Hasn't he got a place?" asked the deacon, pricking up his ears. "I heard he was in a store in New York."

"He lost his place," said Mr. Pomeroy, reluctantly, "partly because of the dullness of general trade."

"Then he can't maintain his sister. She will have to go to the poorhouse. Will you ask her to get ready, and I'll take her right over to the poorhouse."

There was no alternative. Mr. Pomeroy went into the house, and broke the sad news to his wife and Grace.

"Never mind," she said, with attempted cheerfulness, though her lips quivered, "I shan't have to stay there long. Frank will be sure to send for me very shortly."

"It's too bad, Grace," said Sam, looking red about the eyes; "it's too bad that you should have to go to the poorhouse."

"Come and see me, Sam," said Grace.

"Yes, I will, Grace. I'll come often, too. You shan't stay there long."

"Good-by," said Grace, faltering. "You have all been very kind to me."

"Good-by, my dear child," said Mrs. Pomeroy.

"Who knows but you can return to us when the new house is done?"

So poor Grace went out from her pleasant home to find the deacon, grim-faced and stern, waiting for her.

"Jump in, little girl," he said. "You've kept me waiting for you a long time, and my time is valuable."

The distance to the poorhouse was about a mile and a half. For the first half mile Deacon Pinkerton kept silence. Then he began to speak, in a tone of cold condescension, as if it were a favor for such a superior being to address an insignificant child, about to become a pauper.

"Little girl, have you heard from your brother lately?"

"Not very lately, sir."

"What is he doing?"

"He is in a store."

"I apprehend you are mistaken. He has lost his place. He has been turned away," said the deacon, with satisfaction.

"Frank turned away! Oh, sir, you must be mistaken."

"Mr. Pomeroy told me. He found out yesterday when he went to the city."

Poor Grace! she could not longer doubt now, and her brother's misfortune saddened her even more than her own.

"Probably you will soon see your brother."

"Oh, do you think so, sir?" asked Grace, joyfully.

"Yes," answered the deacon, grimly. "He will find himself in danger of starvation in the city, and he'll creep back, only too glad to obtain a nice, comfortable home in the poorhouse."

But Grace knew her brother better than that. She knew his courage, his self-reliance and his independent spirit, and she was sure the deacon was mistaken.

The home for which Grace was expected to be so grateful was now in sight. It was a dark, neglected looking house, situated in the midst of barren fields, and had a lonely and desolate aspect. It was superintended by Mr. and Mrs. Chase, distant relations of Deacon Pinkerton.

Mr. Chase was an inoffensive man, but Mrs. Chase had a violent temper. She was at work in the kitchen when Deacon Pinkerton drove up. Hearing the sound of wheels, she came to the door.

"Mrs. Chase," said the deacon, "I've brought you a little girl, to be placed under your care."

"What's her name?" inquired the lady.

"Grace Fowler."

"Grace, humph! Why didn't she have a decent name?"

"You can call her anything you like," said the deacon.

"Little girl, you must behave well," said Deacon Pinkerton, by way of parting admonition. "The town expects it. I expect it. You must never cease to be grateful for the good home which it provides you free of expense."

Grace did not reply. Looking in the face of her future task-mistress was scarcely calculated to awaken a very deep feeling of gratitude.

"Now," said Mrs. Chase, addressing her new boarder, "just take off your things, Betsy, and make yourself useful."

"My name isn't Betsy, ma'am."

"It isn't, isn't it?"

"No; it is Grace."

"You don't say so! I'll tell you one thing, I shan't allow anybody to contradict me here, and your name's got to be Betsy while you're in this house. Now take off your things and hang them up on that peg. I'm going to set you right to work."

"Yes, ma'am," said Grace, alarmed.

"There's some dishes I want washed, Betsy, and I won't have you loitering over your work, neither."

"Very well, ma'am."

Such was the new home for which poor Grace was expected to be grateful.

Chapter-XIX

What Frank Heard Through the Crevice

Frank looked with some surprise at the woman who was looking through the slide of his door. He had expected to see Nathan Graves. She also regarded him with interest.

"I have brought you some supper," she said.

Frank reached out and drew in a small waiter, containing a cup of tea and a plate of toast.

"Thank you," he said. "Where is the man who brought me here?"

"He has gone out."

"Do you know why he keeps me here in confinement?"

"No," said the woman, hastily. "I know nothing. I see much, but I know nothing."

"Are many prisoners brought here as I have been?" asked our hero, in spite of the woman's refusal to speak.

"No."

"I can't understand what object they can have in detaining me. If I were rich, I might guess, but I am poor. I am compelled to work for my daily bread, and have been out of a place for two weeks."

"I don't understand," she said, in a low voice, rather to herself than to him. "But I cannot wait. I must not stand here. I will come up in fifteen minutes, and if you wish another cup of tea, or some toast, I will bring them."

His confinement did not affect his appetite, for he enjoyed his tea and toast; and when, as she had promised, the woman came up, he told her he would like another cup of tea, and some more toast.

"Will you answer one question?" asked our hero.

"I don't know," answered the woman in a flurried tone.

"You look like a good woman. Why do you stay in such a house as this?"

"I will tell you, though I should do better to be silent. But you won't betray me?"

"On no account."

"I was poor, starving, when I had an application to come here. The man who engaged me told me that it was to be a housekeeper, and I had no suspicion of the character of the house—that it was a den of—"

She stopped short, but Frank understood what she would have said.

"When I discovered the character of the house, I would have left but for two reasons. First, I had no other home; next, I had become acquainted with the secrets of the house, and they would have feared that I would reveal them. I should incur great risk. So I stayed."

Here there was a sound below. The woman started.

"Some one has come," she said. "I must go down I will come up as soon as I can with the rest of your supper."

"Thank you. You need not hurry."

Our hero was left to ponder over what he had heard. There was evidently a mystery connected with this lonely house a mystery which he very much desired to solve. But there was one chance. Through the aperture in the closet he might both see and hear something, provided any should meet there that evening.

The remainder of his supper was brought him by the same woman, but she was in haste, and he obtained no opportunity of exchanging another word with her.

Frank did not learn who it was that had arrived. Listening intently, he thought he heard some sounds in the next room. Opening the closet door, and applying his eye to the aperture, he saw two men seated in the room, one of whom was the man who had brought him there.

He applied his ear to the opening, and heard the following conversation:

"I hear you've brought a boy here, Nathan," said the other, who was a stout, low-browed man, with an evil look.

"Yes," said Graves, with a smile; "I am going to board him here a while."

"What's it all about? What are you going to gain by it?"

"I'll tell you all I know. I've known something of the family for a long time. John Wade employed me long ago. The old millionaire had a son who went abroad and died there. His cousin, John Wade, brought home his son—a mere baby—the old man's grandson, of course, and sole heir, or likely to be, to the old man's wealth, if he had lived. In that case, John Wade would have been left out in the cold, or put off with a small bequest."

"Yes. Did the boy live?"

"No; he died, very conveniently for John Wade, and thus removed the only obstacle from his path."

"Very convenient. Do you think there was any foul play?"

"There may have been."

"But I should think the old man would have suspected."

"He was away at the time. When he returned to the city, he heard from his nephew that the boy was dead. It was a great blow to him, of course. Now, I'll tell you what," said Graves, sinking his voice so that Frank found it difficult to hear, "I'll tell you what I've thought at times."

"I think the grandson may have been spirited off somewhere. Nothing more easy, you know. Murder is a risky operation, and

John Wade is respectable, and wouldn't want to run the risk of a halter."

"You may be right. You don't connect this story of yours with the boy you've brought here, do you?"

"I do," answered Graves, emphatically. "I shouldn't be surprised if this was the very boy!"

"What makes you think so?"

"First, because there's some resemblance between the boy and the old man's son, as I remember him. Next, it would explain John Wade's anxiety to get rid of him. It's my belief that John Wade has recognized in this boy the baby he got rid of fourteen years ago, and is afraid his uncle will make the same discovery."

Frank left the crevice through which he had received so much information in a whirl of new and bewildering thoughts.

"Was it possible," he asked himself, "that he could be the grandson of Mr. Wharton, his kind benefactor?"

Chapter-XX
The Escape

It was eight o'clock the next morning before Frank's breakfast was brought to him.

"I am sorry you have had to wait," the housekeeper said, as she appeared at the door with a cup of coffee and a plate of beefsteak and toast, "I couldn't come up before."

"Have the men gone away?" said Frank.

"Yes."

"Then I have something to tell you. I learned something about myself last night. I was in the closet, and heard the man who brought me here talking to another person. May I tell you the story?"

"If you think it will do any good," said the housekeeper, "but I can't help you if that is what you want."

He told the whole story. As he proceeded, the housekeeper betrayed increased, almost eager interest, and from time to time asked him questions in particular as to the personal appearance of John Wade. When Frank had described him as well as he could, she said, in an excited manner:

"Yes, it is—it must be the same man."

"The same man!" repeated our hero, in surprise.

"Do you know anything about him?"

"I know that he is a wicked man. I am afraid that I have helped him carry out his wicked plan, but I did not know it at the time, or I never would have given my consent."

"I don't understand you," said our hero, puzzled.

"Will you tell me what you mean?"

"Fourteen years ago I was very poor—poor and sick besides. My husband had died, leaving me nothing but the care of a young infant, whom it was necessary for me to support besides myself. Enfeebled by sickness, I was able to earn but little, but we lived in a wretched room in a crowded tenement house. My infant boy was taken sick and died. As I sat sorrowfully beside the bed on which he lay dead, I heard a knock at the door. I opened it, and admitted a man whom I afterward learned to be John Wade. He very soon explained his errand. He agreed to take my poor boy, and pay all the expenses of his burial in Greenwood Cemetery, provided I would not object to any of his arrangements. He was willing besides to pay me two hundred dollars for the relief of my necessities. Though I was almost beside myself with grief for my child's loss, and though this was a very favorable proposal, I hesitated. I could not understand why a stranger should make me such an offer. I asked him the reason."

"'You ask too much,' he answered, appearing annoyed. 'I have made you a fair offer. Will you accept it, or will you leave your child to have a pauper's funeral?'

"That consideration decided me. For my child's sake I agreed to his proposal, and forebore to question him further. He provided a handsome rosewood casket for my dear child, but upon the silver plate was inscribed a name that was strange to me—the name of Francis Wharton."

"Francis Wharton!" exclaimed Frank.

"I was too weak and sorrowful to make opposition, and my baby was buried as Francis Wharton. Not only this, but a monument is erected over him at Greenwood, which bears this name."

She proceeded after a pause:

"I did not then understand his object. Your story makes it clear. I think that you are that Francis Wharton, under whose name my boy was buried."

"How strange!" said Frank, thoughtfully. "I cannot realize it. But how did you know the name of the man who called upon you?"

"A card slipped from his pocket, which I secured without his knowledge."

"How fortunate that I met you," said Frank. "I mean to let Mr. Wharton know all that I have learned, and then he shall decide whether he will recognize me or not as his grandson."

"I have been the means of helping to deprive you of your just rights, though unconsciously. Now that I know the wicked conspiracy in which I assisted, I will help undo the work."

"Thank you," said Frank. "The first thing is to get out of this place."

"I cannot open the door of your room. They do not trust me with the key."

"The windows are not very high from the ground. I can get down from the outside."

"I will bring you a clothesline and a hatchet."

Frank received them with exultation.

"Before I attempt to escape," he said, "tell me where I can meet you in New York. I want you to go with me to Mr. Wharton's. I shall need you to confirm my story."

"I will meet you to-morrow at No. 15 B—Street."

"Then we shall meet to-morrow. What shall I call your name?"

"Mrs. Parker."

"Thank you. I will get away as quickly as possible, and when we are in the city we will talk over our future plans."

With the help of the hatchet, Frank soon demolished the lower part of the window. Fastening the rope to the bedstead, he got out of the window and safely descended to the ground.

A long and fatiguing walk lay before him. But at last he reached the cars, and half an hour later the ferry at Jersey City.

Frank thought himself out of danger for the time being, but he was mistaken.

Standing on the deck of the ferryboat, and looking back to the pier from which he had just started, he met the glance of a man who had intended to take the same boat, but had reached the pier just too late. His heart beat quicker when he recognized in the belated passenger his late jailer, Nathan Graves.

Carried away by his rage and disappointment, Nathan Graves clenched his fist and shook it at his receding victim.

Our hero walked into the cabin. He wanted a chance to deliberate. He knew that Nathan Graves would follow him by the next boat, and it was important that he should not find him. Where was he to go?

Fifteen minutes after Frank set foot on the pier, his enemy also landed. But now the difficult part of the pursuit began. He had absolutely no clew as to the direction which Frank had taken.

For an hour and a half he walked the streets in the immediate neighborhood of the square, but his labor was without reward. Not a glimpse could he catch of his late prisoner.

"I suppose I must go to see Mr. Wade," he at last reluctantly decided. "He may be angry, but he can't blame me. I did my best. I couldn't stand guard over the young rascal all day."

The address which the housekeeper had given Frank was that of a policeman's family in which she was at one time a boarder. On giving his reference, he was hospitably received, and succeeded in making arrangements for a temporary residence.

About seven o'clock Mrs. Parker made her appearance. She was fatigued by her journey and glad to rest.

"I was afraid you might be prevented from coming," said Frank.

"I feared it also. I was about to start at twelve o'clock, when, to my dismay, one of the men came home. He said he had the headache. I was obliged to make him some tea and toast. He remained about till four o'clock, when, to my relief, he went upstairs to lie down. I was afraid some inquiry might be made about you, and your absence discovered, especially as the rope was still hanging out of the window, and I was unable to do anything more than cut off the lower end of it. When the sick man retired to his bed I instantly left the house, fearing that the return of some other of the band might prevent my escaping altogether."

"Suppose you had met one of them, Mrs. Parker?"

"I did. It was about half a mile from the house."

"Did he recognize you?"

"Yes. He asked in some surprise where I was going. I was obliged to make up a story about our being out of sugar. He accepted it without suspicion, and I kept on. I hope I shall be forgiven for the lie. I was forced to it."

"You met no further trouble?"

"No."

"I must tell you of my adventure," said Frank.

"I came across the very man whom I most dreaded—the man who made me a prisoner."

"Since he knows that you have escaped, he is probably on your track," said Mrs. Parker. "It will be hardly safe for you to go to Mr. Wharton's."

"Why?"

"He will probably think you likely to go there, and be lying in wait somewhere about."

"But I must go to Mr. Wharton," said Frank. "I must tell him this story."

"It will be safer to write."

"The housekeeper, Mrs. Bradley, or John Wade, will get hold of the letter and suppress it. I don't want to put them on their guard."

"You are right. It is necessary to be cautious."

"You see I am obliged to call on my grandfather, that is, on Mr. Wharton."

"I can think of a better plan."

"What is it?"

"Go to a respectable lawyer. Tell him your story, and place your case in his hands. He will write to your grandfather, inviting him to call at his office on business of importance, without letting him know what is the nature of it. You and I can be there to meet him, and tell our story. In this way John Wade will know nothing, and learn nothing, of your movements."

"That is good advice, Mrs. Parker, but there is one thing you have not thought of," said our hero.

"What is that?"

"Lawyers charge a great deal for their services, and I have no money."

"You have what is as good a recommendation—a good case. The lawyer will see at once that if not at present rich, you stand a good chance of obtaining a position which will make you so. Besides, your grandfather will be willing, if he admits your claim, to recompense the lawyer handsomely."

"I did not think of that. I will do as you advise to-morrow."

Chapter-XXI
John Wade's Disappointment

Mr. Wharton sat at dinner with his nephew and the housekeeper. He had been at home for some time, and of course on his arrival had been greeted with the news of our hero's perfidy. But, to the indignation of Mrs. Bradley and John, he was obstinately incredulous.

"There is some mistake, I am sure," he said. "Such a boy as Frank is incapable of stealing. You may be mistaken after all, John. Why did you not let him stay till I got back? I should like to have examined him myself."

"I was so angry with him for repaying your kindness in such a way that I instantly ordered him out of the house."

"I blame you, John, for your haste," said his uncle. "It was not just to the boy."

"I acted for the best, sir," he forced himself to say in a subdued tone.

"Young people are apt to be impetuous, and I excuse you; but you should have waited for my return. I will call at Gilbert & Mack's, and inquire of Frank himself what explanation he has to give."

"Of course, sir, you will do what you think proper," said his nephew.

This ended the conversation, and Mr. Wharton, according to his declared intention, went to Gilbert & Mack's. He returned disappointed with the information that our hero was no longer in the store.

I now return to Mr. Wharton at dinner.

"Here is a letter for you, sir," said the housekeeper. "It was brought by the postman this afternoon."

Mr. Wharton adjusted his spectacles and read as follows:

"No.— Wall Street.

"Dear Sir: Will you have the kindness to call at my office to-morrow morning at eleven o'clock, if it suits your convenience? I have an important communication to make to you, which will, I think be of an agreeable character. Should the time named not suit you, will you have the kindness to name your own time?

"Yours respectfully,

"MORRIS HALL."

"Read that, John," said his uncle, passing him the letter.

"Morris Hall is a lawyer, I believe, sir," said John.

"Have you any idea of the nature of the communication he desires to make?"

"No idea at all."

"If it would relieve you, sir, I will go in your place," said John, whose curiosity was aroused.

"Thank you, John, but this is evidently a personal matter. I shall go down there to-morrow at the appointed time."

John was far from suspecting that the communication related to Frank, though he had heard the day previous from Nathan Graves of the boy's escape. He had been very much annoyed, and had given his agent a severe scolding, with imperative orders to recapture the boy, if possible.

It was not without a feeling of curiosity that Mr. Wharton entered the law office of Mr. Hall. He announced himself and was cordially welcomed.

"You have a communication to make to me," said Mr. Wharton.

"I have."

"Tell me all without delay."

"I will, sir. This is the communication I desire to make."

The story of John Wade's treachery was told, and the means by which he had imposed upon his uncle, but the lawyer carefully abstained from identifying the lost grandson with Frank Fowler.

When the story was concluded, Mr. Wharton said:

"Where is my grandson—my poor George's boy? Find him for me, and name your own reward."

"I will show him to you at once, sir. Frank!"

At the word, Frank, who was in an inner office, entered. Mr. Wharton started in amazement.

"Frank!" he exclaimed. "My dear boy, is it you who are my grandson?"

"Grandfather!"

Mr. Wharton held out his arms, and our hero, already attached to him for his kindness, was folded in close embrace.

"Then you believe I am your grandson?" said Frank.

"I believe it without further proof."

"Still, Mr. Wharton," said the lawyer, "I want to submit my whole proof. Mrs. Parker!"

Mrs. Parker entered and detailed her part in the plot, which for fourteen years had separated Frank from his family.

"Enough!" said Mr. Wharton. "I am convinced—I did not believe my nephew capable of such baseness. Mrs. Parker, you shall not regret your confession. I will give you a pension which will relieve you from all fear of want. Call next week on Mr. Hall, and you shall learn what provision I have made for you. You, Frank, will return with me."

"What will Mr. John say?" asked Frank.

"He shall no longer sleep under my roof," said Mr. Wharton, sternly.

Frank was taken to a tailor and fitted out with a handsome new suit, ready-made for immediate use, while three more were ordered.

When Mr. Wharton reached home, he entered the library and rang the bell.

To the servant who answered he said:

"Is Mr. John at home?"

"Yes, sir; he came in ten minutes ago."

"Tell him I wish to see him at once in the library. Summon the housekeeper, also."

Surprised at the summons, John Wade answered it directly. He and Mrs. Bradley met at the door and entered together. Their surprise and dismay may be conjectured when they saw our hero seated beside Mr. Wharton, dressed like a young gentleman.

"John Wade," said his uncle, sternly, "the boy whom you malign, the boy you have so deeply wronged, has found a permanent home in this house."

"What, sir! you take him back?"

"I do. There is no more fitting place for him than the house of his grandfather."

"His grandfather!" exclaimed his nephew and the housekeeper, in chorus.

"I have abundant proof of the relationship. This morning I have listened to the story of your treachery. I have seen the woman whose son, represented to me as my grandson, lies in Greenwood Cemetery. I have learned your wicked plans to defraud him of his inheritance, and I tell you that you have failed."

"I shall make my will to-morrow, bequeathing all my property to my grandson, excepting only an annual income of two thousand dollars to yourself. And now I must trouble you to find a boarding place. After what has passed I do not desire to have you in the family."

"I do not believe he is your grandson," said John Wade, too angry to heed prudential considerations.

"Your opinion is of little consequence."

"Then, sir, I have only to wish you good-morning. I will send for my trunks during the day."

"Good-morning," said Mr. Wharton, gravely, and John Wade left the room, baffled and humiliated.

"I hope, sir," said the housekeeper, alarmed for her position; "I hope you don't think I knew Mr. Frank was your grandson. I never was so astonished and flustrated in my life. I hope you won't discharge me, sir—me that have served you so faithfully for many years."

"You shall remain on probation. But if Frank ever has any fault to find with you, you must go."

"I hope you will forgive me, Mr. Frank."

"I forgive you freely," said our hero, who was at a generous disposition.

Chapter-XXII
Conclusion

Meanwhile poor Grace had fared badly at the poorhouse in Crawford. It was a sad contrast to the gentle and kindly circle at Mr. Pomeroy's. What made it worse for Grace was, that she could hear nothing of Frank. She feared he was sick, or had met with some great misfortune, which prevented his writing.

One day a handsome carriage drove up to the door. From it descended our hero, elegantly attired. He knocked at the door.

Mrs. Chase, who was impressed by wealth, came to the door in a flutter of respect, induced by the handsome carriage.

"What do you wish, sir?" she asked, not recognizing Frank.

"Miss Grace Fowler!" repeated Mrs. Chase, almost paralyzed at Grace being called for by such stylish acquaintances.

"Yes, my sister Grace."

"What! are you Frank Fowler?"

"Yes. I have come to take Grace away."

"I don't know as I have the right to let her go," said Mrs. Chase, cautiously, regretting that Grace was likely to escape her clutches.

"Here is an order from Deacon Pinkerton, chairman of the overseers of the poor."

"That is sufficient. She can go. You look as if you had prospered in the city," she added, with curiosity.

"Yes. I have found my grandfather, who is very wealthy."

"You don't say!" ejaculated Mrs. Chase. "I'll tell Grace at once."

Grace at work in the kitchen had not heard of the arrival. What was her surprise when Mrs. Chase, entering the room, said, graciously:

"Go up at once, Grace, and change your clothes. Your brother has come for you. He is going to take you away."

Grace almost gasped for breath.

"Is it true?"

"It is indeed. Your brother looks remarkably well. He is rich. He has found a rich grandfather, and has come for you in a carriage."

In amazed bewilderment Grace went upstairs and put on her best dress, poor enough in comparison with her brother's clothes, and was soon happy in his embrace.

"I am glad to see you, my dear child," said Mr. Wharton, who had accompanied Frank. "Will you come to the city and live with me and your brother?"

"Oh, sir, I shall be glad to be wherever Frank is."

"Good-bye, my dear child," sand Mrs. Chase, whose feelings were very much changed, now that Grace was a rich young lady. "Come and see me some time."

"Thank you, Mrs. Chase. Good-bye!"

The carriage rolled on.

A few words only remain. Our hero was placed at a classical school, and in due time entered college, where he acquitted himself with distinction. He is now making a tour of Europe. Grace was also placed at an excellent school, and has developed into a handsome and accomplished young lady. It is thought she will marry Sam Pomeroy, who obtained a place in a counting-room through Mr. Wharton's influence, and is now head clerk, with a prospect of partnership. His father received a gift of five thousand dollars from Mr. Wharton as an acknowledgment of his kindness to Frank. Tom Pinkerton holds a subordinate clerkship in the same house, and is obliged to look up to Sam as his superior. It chafes his pride, but his father has become a poor man, and Tom is too prudent to run the risk of losing his situation. John Wade draws his income regularly, but he is never seen at his uncle's house.

Mr. Wharton is very happy in his grandson, and made happier by the intelligence just received from Europe of Frank's engagement to a brilliant young New York lady whom he met in his travels. He bids fair, though advanced in age, to live some years yet, to witness the happiness of his dear grandson, once a humble cash-boy.